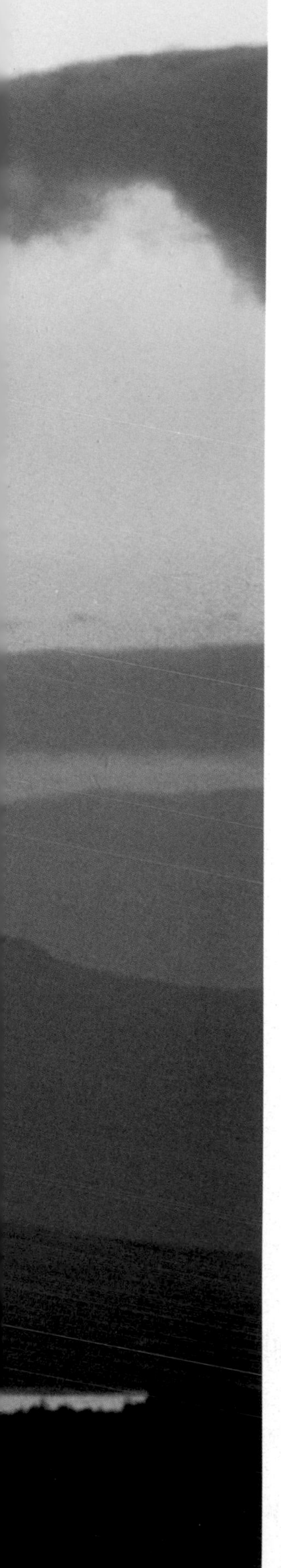

Saints *and* Sea-kings

The First Kingdom of the Scots

Ewan Campbell

Series editor: Gordon Barclay

CANONGATE BOOKS
with
HISTORIC SCOTLAND

THE MAKING OF SCOTLAND

Series editor:
Gordon Barclay

Other titles available:

WILD HARVESTERS
The First People in Scotland

FARMERS, TEMPLES AND TOMBS
Scotland in the Neolithic and Early Bronze Age

SETTLEMENT AND SACRIFICE
The Later Prehistoric People of Scotland

A GATHERING OF EAGLES
Scenes from Roman Scotland

THE SEA ROAD
A Viking Voyage through Scotland

SURVIVING IN SYMBOLS
A Visit to the Pictish Nation

ANGELS, FOOLS AND TYRANTS
Britons and Anglo-Saxons in Southern Scotland
AD 450–750

First published in Great Britain in 1999
by Canongate Books Ltd, 14 High Street,
Edinburgh EH1 1TE

British Library Cataloguing-in-Publication Data
A catalogue record for this book is available on request
from the British Library

ISBN 0 86241 874 7

Series Design:
James Hutcheson, Canongate Books
Design:
Design Associates

Printed in Spain by
Mateu Cromo, Madrid

Previous page
Sunset over Jura.
KILMARTIN HOUSE TRUST/DAVID LYONS

Contents

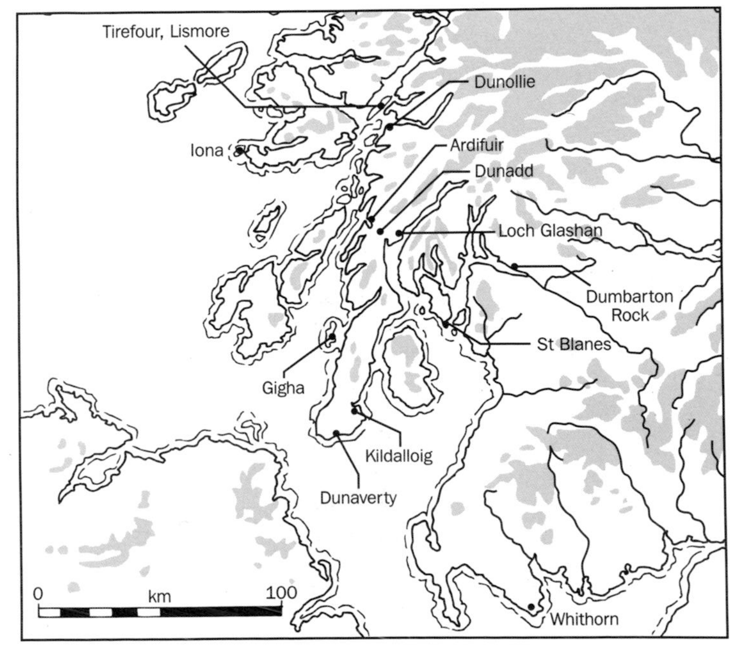

Location Map
This map shows the location of sites mentioned in the book.
HISTORIC SCOTLAND/ ROB BURNS

Province of the Sea-Kings
Sea and land intermingle in this view up the coast of Argyll.
KILMARTIN HOUSE TRUST/DAVID LYONS

Introduction

Argyll, on the west coast of what is now Scotland, was the original heartland of the Scottish kingdom. In the period covered by this book, roughly AD 400–800, it was inhabited by people who were described as Scots, and their kingdom was known as Dál Riata. This book is an introduction to these people, who lived through one of the most radical periods of change in Scottish history. It is at this time that we encounter the first mention of Scottish kings, the earliest written books, a navy and the first naval battle in Britain, the beginnings of state bureaucracy with a census and tax collection, and the first Christians and the first churches. These developments marked the transition from the tribal societies, which had been in existence for many thousands of years of prehistory, to the type of medieval society which was the foundation of the modern Scottish state. But how did this now rather remote and rugged area become the springboard for the Scottish kingdom? It seems to be appropriate 1500 years later, with the advent of a revived Scottish Parliament, to take a fresh look at these origins in the light of recent archaeological research.

This period of history has been given many names which reflect different people's ideas about the time. For example, it has been called the Dark Ages, the Early Christian period, the Late Celtic, the Early Historic period, the Age of Saints, and the Post-Roman period. We will refer to it by the standard historical term, the early medieval period, as it marks the start of what we call the middle ages which end around AD 1600. The people of Dál Riata are often referred to as Celts, or Scots, but both of these are confusing terms not used by the Dalriadans of themselves in their own language. The term Celtic has been used in so many different ways in the past, sometimes referring to language, an art style, ethnicity or a time period, that archaeologists are wary of using the term. The term *Scotti* was applied by Latin writers to people who spoke Gaelic, but it is probably not a complimentary term (it may mean 'pirates') and is, confusingly, applied to Irish or Scots in Latin writings. It is probably best to refer to the inhabitants of Ireland and Dál Riata as Gaels, as this is what they called themselves – *Goídil* in Old Irish.

Isles of the Saints
The first Christians settled on remote islands, like this isolated monastery and graveyard on the Garvellachs, between Mull and Jura.
KILMARTIN HOUSE TRUST/DAVID LYONS

Old Worlds, New Worlds: From Iron Age Tribes to Medieval state

Sea, land and sky

The visitor to the west coast of Argyll encounters a landscape where the normal boundaries between the elements seem to have dissolved. Sea and land seem inextricably mixed as long fjords bite deep into the mountains and rugged peninsulas reach far out towards the sea, and the sea itself is scattered with

Wooded Hillside
This view of Linne Mhurich shows the difficulty of overland travel in Argyll in the days before proper roads.
KILMARTIN HOUSE TRUST/DAVID LYONS

numerous islands, large and small, seeming to have broken off from the mainland. The air also seems to have become mixed with water, with rain, mists and clouds descending and clearing suddenly from the hilltops, and water cascading down the hillsides in numerous waterfalls and fast-flowing rivers. This interplay of land, sea and air often results in a remarkable quality of light, and no vista ever seems to remain the same for very long. These features lend a magical quality to the landscape, and it is easy to see how the numerous folktales and traditions of the area grew up. Tales of kelpies (water-sprites), islands which appear and disappear, and fairy mounds with entrances to the underworld, do not seem so far-fetched in this landscape.

It is much more difficult for the modern visitor to appreciate how important the sea was to the early inhabitants. Before the coming of modern roads, overland travel was arduous and time-consuming because of the steep wooded slopes and long sea lochs. Even today Dunadd, the royal centre of Dál Riata, is a three-hour drive from Glasgow, though only 45 miles (70km) away as the crow flies. In the eighteenth century, cattle drovers took three days to make the same journey, and the educated Lowland Scots or English of the time thought the western Highlands were as exotic as anywhere in the world. As Dr Johnston put it in 1773 at the time of his own *Tour of the Hebrides:*

> *To the southern inhabitants of Scotland, the state of the mountains and the islands is equally unknown with that of Borneo or Sumatra: of both they have only heard a little, and guess the rest.*

The mountains of the central Highlands were a formidable barrier to communication. Adomnán, abbot of Iona in the late seventh century, described how the Picts of the east were separated from the Scots of the west by *Druim Alban,* 'the spine of Britain'. The Glens of Antrim in northern Ireland, on the other hand, were as close and accessible as Islay or Tiree to the kings of Dál Riata.

Although the sea lochs make the area remote by modern standards, in the early medieval period the sea was the quickest and most convenient means of transport. Argyll is in effect an archipelago, and the sea linked the islands with neighbouring north of Ireland as effectively as the roads of Roman Britain linked towns and cities. The sea, sailors and ships therefore played an essential role in the changes of the time, a role which has often not been appreciated in the past. As we shall see, the growth of trade, the basis of political power and the advent of Christianity were all deeply influenced by the maritime environment.

The end of the Iron Age

To understand the extent of the changes which were to affect early medieval Argyll we have to know something of the preceding prehistoric societies of the region. This was the Iron Age, when iron tools and weapons were in use, and some archaeologists consider that in Ireland, the Highlands and Islands this period continued until as late as the eighth century. The characteristic forms of settlement in western Scotland were stone-walled enclosures, known variously as duns, forts and brochs. However, Argyll differed from other areas of Scotland: it had almost no brochs, the great stone towers which are unique to Scotland; it had many more duns, small subcircular structures lower than brochs; and it had unenclosed houses built on platforms cut out of the hillsides. There therefore seems to have been something different about this area even before the supposed date of the foundation of Dál Riata. One other type of settlement which was found both in the Iron Age and in later periods was the crannog, an artificial island with wooden palisades and buildings.

Iron Age Settlement
The map of Iron Age settlement types shows that Argyll differed from the rest of Scotland in having few brochs and forts.
HISTORIC SCOTLAND/ROB BURNS

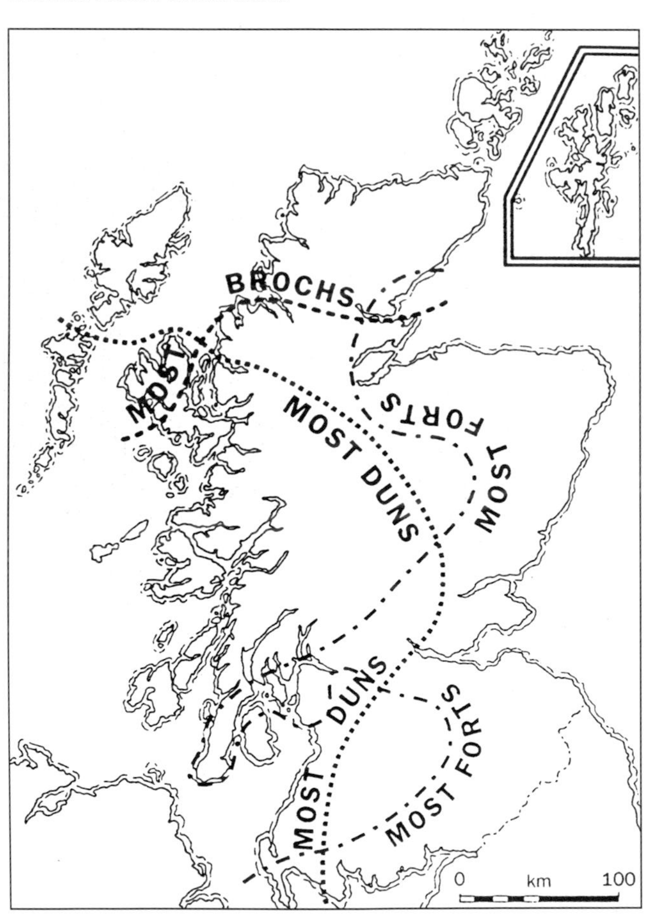

We know little of how society functioned at this period though some clues can be gained from archaeology and a few Roman writers who came into contact with northern 'barbarians'. People were allied to tribal groups, and they had leaders, at least in times of battle. The larger hillforts may have been the residences of these leaders; they may also have been used as communal centres for the exchange of goods and perhaps for ceremonial activities. Religion was probably based on gods and nature elements, and weapons and other material are often found in bogs or watery places where they were placed as offerings to placate the forces of nature. Very few burials are known, and bodies seem to have been treated in what to us appears a callous manner. Some were buried in old houses, others cut up and placed in pits, and some were cremated, but probably most often they were left exposed to the elements until only the bones remained. Some travel occurred between tribes, and some items were exchanged

over long distances, but no sustained trade took place.

While some elements of this society survived into the early medieval period, by AD 800 much had changed. The old religion had been replaced by Christianity, druids by priests, and most burial was in cemeteries or stone-lined cists. Tribal leaders were starting to become dynastic kings of regions rather than heads of

Broch

One of the few brochs in Argyll, Tirefour occupies a commanding site on the island of Lismore.

related tribes, their power and wealth was increasing, and new forms of government were being introduced. Sea-borne trade had begun to develop, and Dál Riata had contacts with neighbouring kingdoms, continental Europe and even the Mediterranean world. Some people still lived in forts, duns and crannogs, but most of these settlements were abandoned within a hundred years of the end of our period, being replaced by open farmsteads and castles.

Myths of Irish origin – history, language and national identity

Traditional stories and genealogies tell how Dál Riata was founded around AD 500 by the Irish king Fergus Mor and his sons, who colonised Argyll from north Antrim, the area of Ireland closest to Scotland. An entry in the Irish Annals of Tigernach states under the year 500:

Fergus Mor, mac Erc, with the nation of Dál Riada, held part of Britain, and died there.

Irish Annals

This entry in the Annals of Tigernach appears to describe the arrival of Fergus Mor around AD 500, but can we take it at face value? It may have been inserted at a later date as the manuscript was partly compiled in the tenth century and written down in the fourteenth century.

THE BODLEIAN LIBRARY, UNIVERSITY OF OXFORD (MS. RAWL B.488, fo. 7r)

The idea that the Scots came from Ireland has been widely accepted since a different version of the story was reported by the English monk Bede in his *Ecclesiastical History of the English People* in the eighth century, and is repeated in every history book.

Britain received a third tribe, ... namely the Irish (Scotti). These came from Ireland under their leader Reuda, and won lands from the Picts...they are still called Dalreudini after this leader.

Neither of these sources is a contemporary record of events. The entry in the Annals of Tigernach belongs to a stratum of the tenth century in a manuscript of the fourteenth century. Bede's account is closer to the events described, but still five hundred years after the supposed date of Reuda (third century). *Scotti* was the word used by Roman authors to describe the inhabitants of Ireland, and the term was later applied to all who spoke Gaelic. The use of the same Latin term for Irish and 'Scots' has caused confusion to generations of schoolchildren, aptly satirised in the spoof history book *1066 and All That:*

The Scots (originally Irish, but by now Scotch) were at this time inhabiting Ireland, having driven the Irish (Picts) out of Scotland; while the Picts (originally Scots) were now Irish (living in brackets) and vice versa.

It seems likely that the word *Scotti* was applied to all people who spoke Gaelic, a branch of the Celtic family of languages which includes modern Irish and Scots Gaelic. This type of Celtic is technically known as Q-Celtic, or Brittonic, to distinguish it from the P-Celtic, or Goidelic, branch which includes Pictish, Welsh, Breton and Cornish. The common language shared by the Irish and the Dalriadic Gaels was taken as

strong support for the idea that the Gaels had come over from Ireland as recounted in the origin tales.

The conventional historical account is that the Scots migrated from Antrim to Argyll either around 500, according to Tigernach, or in the third century AD, according to Bede. They came from a small kingdom called Dál Riata, and the same name was given to their Scottish colony. They ousted a native Pictish population, and settled much of Argyll. By the late sixth century, relations between Scottish and Irish Dál Riata were strained, and a convention was held at Drum Cett to settle the position of the Scottish 'colony' in relation to the overlordship of the overking of Ulster. After this date, probably 574, Scottish Dál Riata was more or less independent.

This picture of Irish colonisation of western Scotland, and eventually most of Scotland, has recently been challenged. If the inhabitants of Dál Riata migrated from Ireland, there should be Irish types of object and forms of settlement in Argyll, but this does not appear to be the case. The commonest form of settlement in Ireland at this time were small circular enclosures with earth banks, known as ringforts, which were probably used for keeping cattle as well as for living accommodation. No ringforts are known in Argyll, although there are suitable locations for them. Some stone-walled ringforts are known in Ireland, but these are not the same as the Scottish duns, which are usually on hilltops. Scientific dating of Argyll duns has shown that the type was in use from the early Iron Age (at least 500 BC) through to the early medieval period, so they cannot have been introduced from Ireland by Fergus. Crannogs are common in Ireland and Scotland, but again recent scientific dating has shown that Scottish crannogs were built from the early Iron Age, while those in Ireland only appear in the sixth century AD. The method used to date the sites, dendrochronology, measures and compares the varying width of tree-rings on timbers from the crannogs, the patterns of wide and narrow rings being dependent on the weather. This evidence suggests that crannogs were invented in Scotland (there are almost none in England or Wales) and later spread to Ireland.

Personal ornaments such as brooches and dress pins were one of the main ways of telling who belonged to what group or tribe. Everyone needed to wear these to fasten their cloaks and tunics, and different designs became associated with different groups. These brooches also came to be badges of different social classes: the Irish documents tell us that a gold brooch was suitable for a king, and a silver one for a noble; most people's brooches were of bronze. The commonest brooch in Dál Riata had rectangular terminals with bevelled edges, but in Ireland the terminals had

Celtic Deity
This stone head of a Celtic pagan deity was found at Appin. The elemental power of this image aptly demonstrates how different Celtic religion was from Christianity.
NATIONAL MUSEUMS OF SCOTLAND

Dress Pins

This map shows the distribution of the commonest type of dress pin in Ireland. Only two of these loop-headed spiral-ring pins are found in Scotland, where different forms of dress fastners were fashionable.

HISTORIC SCOTLAND/ROB BURNS

animal heads. Pins with spiral rings, rather like key-rings, were very common in Ireland, but almost unknown in Scotland.

A type of monument which is distinctively Irish from this period is the ogham pillar. This was a memorial stone erected to commemorate someone. The person's name was inscribed in an alphabet (ogham) invented in Ireland which consisted of stroke marks cut in the stone. Several hundred of these stones are found, in all parts of Ireland, dating from the fifth to seventh centuries, but only two occur in Argyll, not enough to suggest that any number of people crossed from Ireland.

In fact there is almost no archaeological evidence to support the traditional view of migration from Ireland, and some evidence to support the view that there was considerable influence in the *opposite* direction, from Scotland to Ireland. All the evidence points to a continuity of the population in Argyll from the early Iron Age through to the medieval period. How then can we explain the origin tales, and the undeniable fact that Gaelic came to be spoken in Scotland?

Language and identity were closely linked as there was no equivalent of the modern conception of nations and nationality at this time. People saw themselves as belonging to a group of kinfolk, or as descendants of a renowned ancestor, but only as 'Irish' or 'English' in the sense of people who shared a common language. When storytellers recounted tales of a people's origin, it was assumed that all those who spoke a common language must have come from the same place. Other peoples had similar origin legends, some of them patently absurd to our modern ears. The Picts, for example, were said to have sailed from Scythia, and the Britons traced their ancestors back to the Roman Brutus. When the first histories and king-lists came to be written down, these stories were reinforced by the invention of suitable ancestors for kings, often stretching far back into prehistory. Painstaking detective work by modern historians has revealed how these stories and genealogies were often adapted by later rulers to serve their own political purposes. For example, the genealogies in the seventh-century *Senchus Fer nAlban* (the History of the Men of Scotland) were rewritten in the tenth century to incorporate the Fergus story. This was done to try to bolster the claims of one branch of the claimants to the Scottish throne. The first kings of Dál Riata that we can be sure existed were Comgall and Gabrán, who died around 550.

The Dalriadans thought they came from Ireland because they could speak to people there, but not to Picts or Britons on the other side of the Druim Alban. They did not appreciate that language can change over long periods of time, and that the language of people who were in close contact with each other

Ogham Stone
This stone from the island of Gigha is one of only two early examples of this Irish form of writing in Argyll.

would continue to develop in the same direction, while the language of people in other areas would develop in different ways. As Goidelic Celtic is older than Brittonic, it seems that the peoples to the east of Druim Alban shared in the development of Brittonic which was taking place throughout the rest of Britain, while, to the west of Druim Alban, Goidelic remained in use because of the close links with the Gaels of Ireland. There were also political reasons for stressing the Irish origin, as, at least for a time, there was a joint rulership of Scottish and Irish Dál Riata. An origin legend which showed the kings of Dál Riata in Scotland coming from Ireland helped them to claim sovereignty over Irish Dál Riata.

This new version of history sees the 'Scots' of Dál Riata not as immigrant Irish settlers, but as 'Irish' speakers who had always lived in Scotland, and who shared a common language with their Gaelic neighbours. Although the seaways enabled them to have close links with Ireland, they developed their own distinctive culture within Scotland.

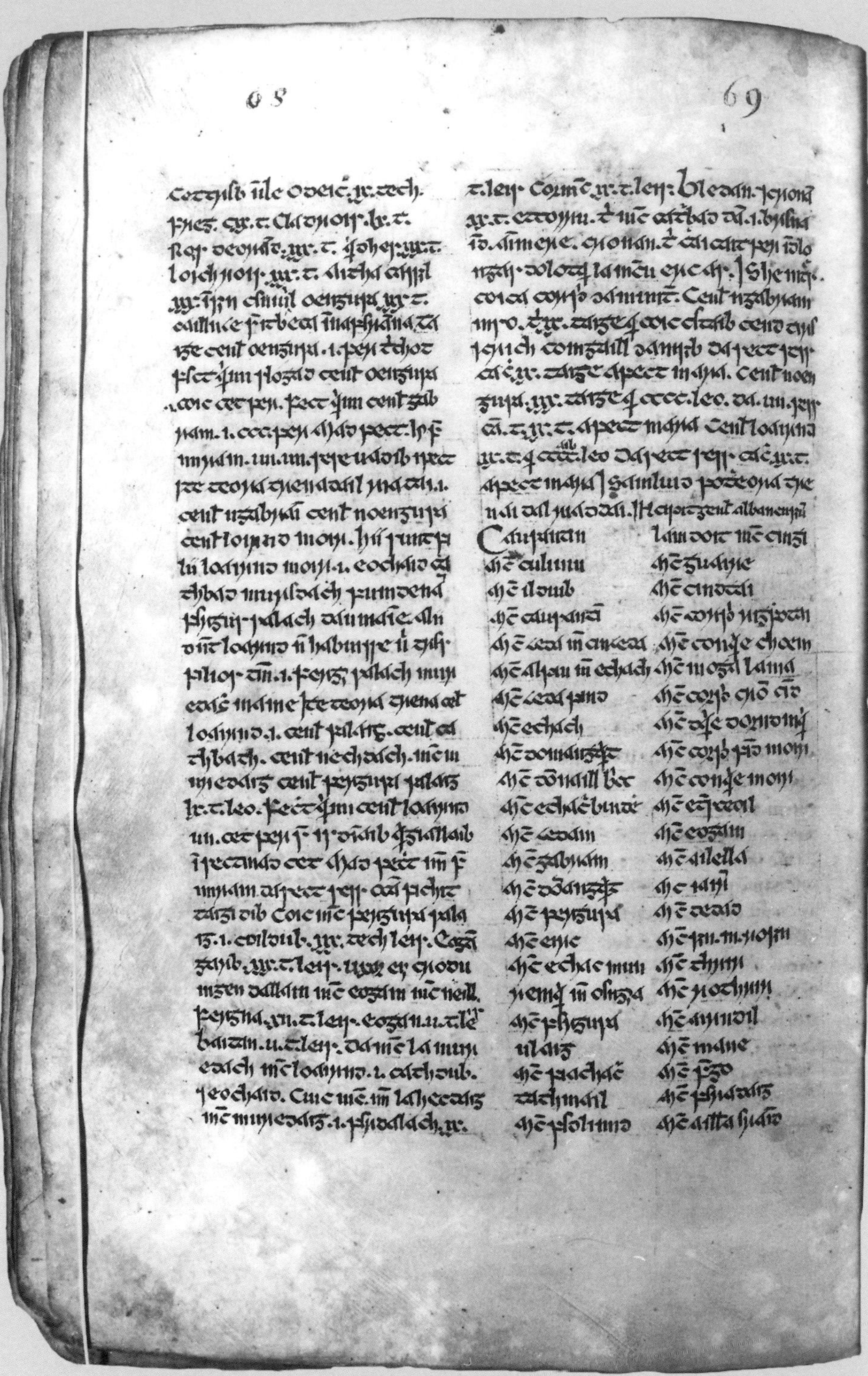

Senchus Fer nAlban

This document was originally compiled in the seventh century as a register of all the households in Dál Riata, and the number of warriors each could muster for the king.

TRINITY COLLEGE, DUBLIN

Living in the Material World

Kin and kings

The way that people related to each other in Dál Riata was very different from society today. People saw themselves as belonging to large extended families which included all descendants of a person's great, great grandfather. Young men and women were often sent to be brought up by foster-parents, providing another network of social ties. These extended families also formed alliances in larger tribal groups. In Dál Riata, we know the names

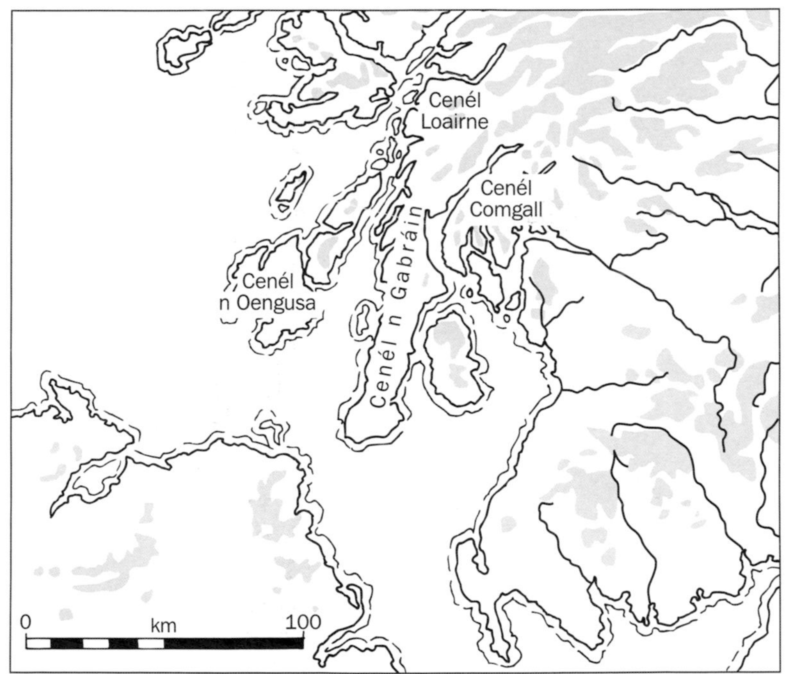

Sub-divisions of Dál Riata
This map shows the approximate areas controlled by the different peoples of Dál Riata. Boundaries were not fixed and varied with the fortunes of each kindred.
HISTORIC SCOTLAND/ROB BURNS

of a number of these kindreds or Cenéla: the Cenél Loairn, Cenél nGabráin, Cenél nOengusa, and Cenél Comgaill. We also know roughly the areas they lived in: the Cenél Loairn in Lorn, the Cenél nGabráin in Kintyre, the Cenél nOengusa in Islay, and the Cenél Comgaill in Cowal.

We have very few documents from this period, but one remarkable survival tells us a great deal about society and even gives us a glimpse of the usually nameless lesser folk of the time. This 'History of the Men of Scotland', in Gaelic *Senchus Fer nAlban,* was compiled originally in the seventh century, though as we have seen it was added to and emended in the tenth century.

Royal Inauguration
A reconstruction of the inauguration of a king of Dál Riata at Dunadd. The king placed his foot in the rock-cut footprint during the ceremony. He is shown accompanied by religious figures, including the abbot of Iona, and surrounded by nobles. The whole scene could be viewed by crowds gathered on the fortified enclosure below.
DAVID HOGG

The *Senchus* was in effect the earliest census known from Britain. Although there is a seventh-century Anglo-Saxon document known as the Tribal Hidage, this merely gives a total figure for each kingdom, and it is not until the Domesday Book of the eleventh century that a more detailed survey was undertaken. In the case of the Cenél Loairn the *Senchus* lists the sub-divisions, the number of households in each and often the name of the head of family. For example, in Lorn:

> *Coildub has thirty houses; Eogan Garb has thirty houses, his wife is Crodu, daughter of Dallán, son of Eogan, son of Niall; Fergna has fifteen houses; Eogan has five houses; Báitán has five houses.*

The purpose of this census was to assess the fighting strength of each area. Each family had to supply a set number of warriors to man the ships which were essential for warfare in the maritime environment of Dál Riata. Each group of twenty houses had to provide 28 oarsmen, enough to man two 'seven-bencher' vessels. The vessels were large sailing currachs, wicker-framed and covered with cow-hide. The navy was therefore the basis of social obligations to the overlord and the king. Many expeditions by the Dalriadan navy are recorded in the early Iona Chronicles, including, in 719, the earliest recorded naval battle in British history. In this case the battle was between the Cenél nGabráin and the Cenél Loairn, but the fleet attacked places as far afield as the Western Isles, Orkney, Skye, the Isle of Man, and Ulster.

Such an organised navy was important not just because it was the basis of the power of the Dalriadan kings, but also because it shows us that Dál Riata had a bureaucracy. The census was probably also used to assess tax or tribute due from each household. The production of the census shows that records were kept, and that there were literate people in the king's retinue capable of writing down the information. This degree of organisation was as advanced as anything in Britain or northern Europe in the seventh century, and shows that Dál Riata cannot be regarded as at all backward in the process of developing a medieval state.

These obligations of the populace to provide the king with service and tribute required a reciprocal obligation on the part of the king, who gave protection to his subjects and also judged disputes between neighbours and kinsfolk at periodic assemblies and fairs. He also gave back to his subjects some of the wealth they gave to him, by holding feasts and giving them gifts. Unlike later medieval kings, kings of Dál Riata did not make laws, nor did they become kings purely by accident of birth. Kings were chosen from a group of nobles who were part of the royal extended family, but son did not necessarily succeed father. There

is even the suggestion that, in cases of dispute, lots were cast to choose the new king.

The king was looked on as a symbol of the people in a pre-Christian manner, though the Church tried to combat this aspect and make the king more like the image of an Old Testament ruler such as David or Solomon. During his inauguration, the king underwent a ceremony representing his marriage to the land. By placing his foot in a footprint carved in the living rock he signalled his dominion over the land, and at the same time his dependence on it for support and nurture for his people. Several

Royal Carvings
This footprint carved in the rock on top of Dunadd was used in the inauguration ceremonies of the kings of Dál Riata. The ogham inscription has recently been translated and shown to be Gaelic, not Pictish as once believed.

of these inauguration sites are known in Ireland, and the most important one in Dál Riata was at Dunadd.

On the summit of this rocky crag there are other carvings associated with inauguration – a carved boar, a rock-cut basin possibly for libations, an inscription in a type of writing (ogham) invented in Ireland, and possibly a rock-cut throne. The whole site is imbued with a vision of the power of the landscape and of the ancestors. When standing on the footprint, on a clear day, the sharp peak of Cruachan, the sacred mountain of Argyll, is just visible above the skyline of the local hills. The king himself would be silhouetted on the skyline of the crag from the viewpoint of the crowds gathered to watch the ceremony on the terraces below the summit. Surrounding Dunadd is one of the densest concentrations of earlier prehistoric burial monuments in Britain, including the only henge and cursus on the west coast, a stone circle, chambered cairns, numerous Bronze Age cairns, standing stones, cist burials, and rock carvings. The choice of this setting for the inauguration of the Dalriadic kings was deliberate, intended to emphasise the links with the past and show that the kings were part of this ancient landscape.

Everyday life

Duns, forts and crannogs are the only structures that we know were lived in at this time. As there are only a few hundred of them scattered around Argyll, they must have been the houses of the upper echelons of society, the nobles and important freemen. We have no idea how the majority of people lived, though some may have inhabited the many small ruined houses whose grass-covered foundations can be seen in many areas. These are usually thought to be post-medieval and to have been deserted at the time of the Clearances, but very similar structures in Pictland have turned out to belong to this period.

The smaller circular duns would have been roofed with structures like wig-wams, probably covered with heather or turf thatch. Within this house, the family would have lived communally, their daily lives differing little from their prehistoric ancestors. Hand-turned stone querns are one of the few items usually found on these sites. These were used to grind grain grown in the small patches of better soil which can be found amongst the rocky outcrops on the hillsides. In Ireland and the Northern Isles watermills of an early type with horizontal wheels

Dun

This well-preserved dun at Ardifuir near Dunadd was built in the Iron Age but continued to be occupied in the early medieval period. It is unusual in being in a valley rather than a hilltop. It may have acted as a lookout station for Dunadd as it has extensive views down the Sound of Jura.

KILMARTIN HOUSE TRUST/DAVID LYONS

were introduced in the seventh century, but none are known from mainland Scotland. The cereals grown were barley and oats, both suited to the climatic conditions on the west coast. Charred grains from seventh-century layers at Dunadd show that oats were the main crop there, grown on the gravel terraces of the Kilmartin valley. This is one of the earliest recorded instances of oats in Britain, which may have been brought from the continent. So at least one stereotype applied to the early Scots – they did eat porridge!

The agricultural economy may have been based on cattle, which were well suited to graze on the rough pasture and boggy meadows of the hills and valleys. Cattle bones show that the animals were about half the size of a modern cow, and were probably similar in breed to the Highland Black or Kyloe cattle

Hoard of Querns
The large number of corn-grinding querns found at Dunadd shows that there was large-scale processing of grain at the site.
RCAHMS: CROWN COPYRIGHT

which used to be driven from Argyll to the Lowlands in the eighteenth century to feed the growing urban population. Pigs and sheep were also kept, and wild resources such as salmon, deer and shell-fish would have been used to some extent.

Forts and larger duns may have been the residences of princes and royal families. Several of these forts are mentioned by name in the early annals, sometimes in association with royalty. These include Dunollie, Dunadd, Tarbert, Loch Fyne, Dunaverty and the unlocated Creich. Dunollie and Dunadd have both been excavated and dateable finds show they were occupied in the early medieval period. We shall see many of the finds from Dunadd in later sections of this book, but the variety of objects, along with the inauguration footprint, and the other symbols, all show that Dunadd was the main royal fort of Dál Riata. The fort sits on a craggy outcrop and has a series of terraces enclosed by stone ramparts. It seems to have started as a small dun on the summit in the fifth century, and was gradually enlarged over the next few centuries. The fort itself was not necessarily the residence of the king, as he may have spent his time travelling

Dunadd
This plan, based on evidence from recent excavations, shows how Dunadd grew from a small hilltop Dun in the Iron age to become a large fort in the early medieval period.
HOWARD MASON

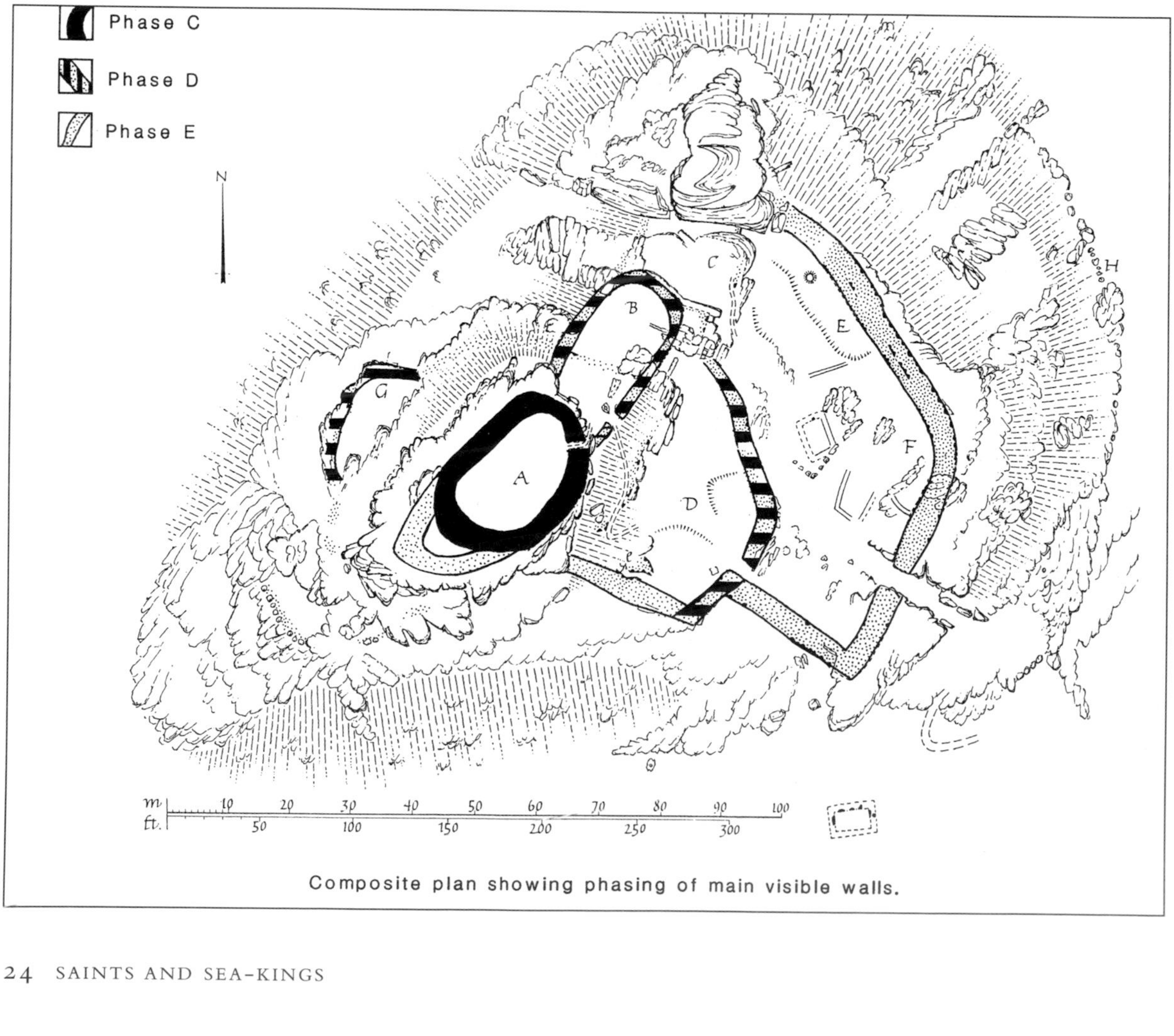

Phase C
Phase D
Phase E
N
A B C D E F G H
m 10 20 30 40 50 60 70 80 90 100
ft. 50 100 150 200 250 300

Composite plan showing phasing of main visible walls.

Brooch Making
Excavations at Dunadd showed there was a metalworking workshop there in the seventh century, producing broochs and other jewellery in precious metals.
DAVID HOGG

around his lands, receiving tributes and holding feasts, but it was used for ceremonial purposes. Large quantities of moulds and crucibles were found at Dunadd, left over from the manufacture of fine brooches, and traces of gold and silver on crucibles make it certain that brooches of precious metal were made here. The king would give these brooches as gifts to his followers, who would wear them as badges of their rank in society. Feasts were held by the king using the tribute of agricultural produce he received from the farmers, and wine from the continent would be served in fine glass vessels brought by Gaulish traders. The king's control over the production of fine brooches, and over access to imported luxuries, was used as a means of keeping his nobles under obligation to him, making them less likely to rebel.

Loch Glashan Crannog
DAVID HOGG

Loch Glashan

The tiny artificial island (crannog) in Loch Glashan gives a unique glimpse into everyday life in Dál Riata. The waterlogged conditions have preserved many organic items which decay and disappear on most archae-ological sites. Hundreds of pieces of leather were found, indicating that the major activity here was leather-working. The most unusual find was a leather jerkin, and there were also shoes, a knife sheath and many offcuts from the production of other items. The many wooden items found included bowls and troughs which were used instead of pottery in most of western Scotland, along with a spoon, a paddle, a bucket and a spindle-whorl. Continental pottery of the same type as found at Dunadd, and a brooch with amber insets, points to a high status and links to the royal site 8km down the Add valley. It may be that the leather goods made here were traded for some of the imported goods which came to Dunadd.

Wooden Bowl
Wood rather than pottery was used for kitchen utensils. This bowl is from Loch Glashan crannog.
GLASGOW MUSEUMS AND ART GALLERIES

We do not know what sort of buildings were erected within these forts, as only the turf-walled bothies of the metalworkers have been recognised. Certainly there is no sign of the large rectangular timber halls which are a feature of Anglo-Saxon and British royal sites.

Crannogs were the other type of site in use. To build these artificial islands needed large resources of timber, and many labourers. Only important nobles could command these resources, and some crannogs may have belonged to kings. One such is in Loch Glashan, which lies a few kilometres up the River Add from Dunadd, and was revealed when the loch level was lowered in the 1960s.

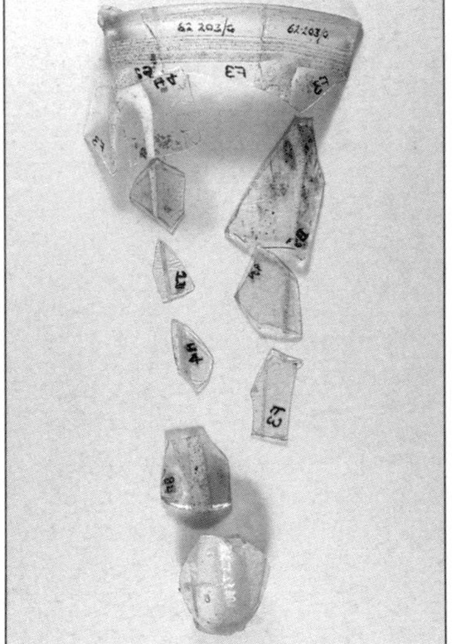

Glass Beaker
Drinking beakers like this one found in Wales were imported to Dál Riata from western France. These fragile and expensive vessels were used to serve wine in feasts at aristocratic sites.
EWAN CAMPBELL

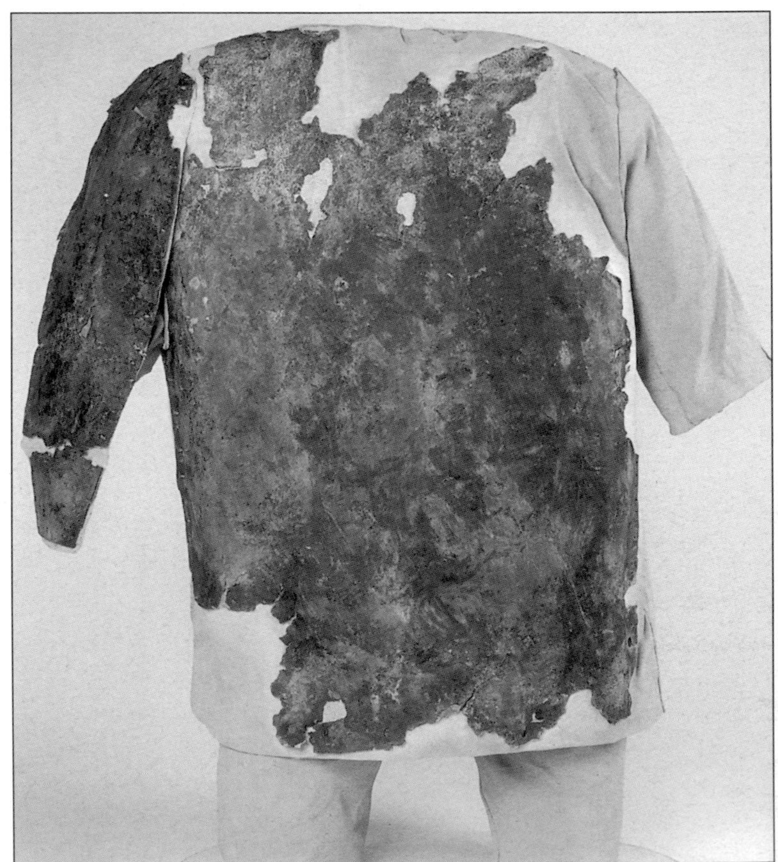

Leather Jerkin
This unique garment from Loch Glashan crannog was just one of many leather items found preserved in the silts of the loch. Such items almost never survive on archaeological sites.
GLASGOW MUSEUMS AND ART GALLERIES

Dunadd in the mist
KILMARTIN HOUSE TRUST/DAVID LYONS

The Inner World

New beliefs

One of the most profound changes to occur in early medieval Scotland was the advent of Christianity. Although Christianity was of great significance to individuals in terms of their own inner spirituality, it is the effects on society which are easier to see from the archaeological remains and historical records. Christianity brought with it new ideas, artefacts and technologies which were to contribute to the transformation of not just the inner landscape of the mind, but also the outer physical landscape and even the ways in which people related to each other. Without Christianity we would not have had books at this period, or the history that written documents tell us; we would not have the great art expressed in the illuminated manuscripts such as the Book of Kells, or the imposing and intricate sculpture of the high crosses, or the fine metalwork of the Ardagh Chalice; we would not have the great monasteries such as Iona, or important figures such as Columba and Adomnán.

Other changes are less obvious, but just as important. The early Church encouraged a new view of kingship which contributed to the development of a unified Scotland. The way people treated their dead changed dramatically with burial in enclosed cemeteries. The new technologies included techniques of building rectangular wooden and later stone structures; new types of plough which allowed new areas of cultivation; and the introduction of water-mills. The Church itself, as an institution which could own land and accumulate wealth, was a novel idea in a society where after death all the wealth of an individual was divided equally amongst the person's heirs, and even a king did not pass his land to his son. The new Christian leaders therefore became very powerful figures in society, controlling many aspects of life previously the realm of the *filid* (seers) or druids. One of the most intriguing aspects of this change in power is to find an explanation of how these ascetic Christians persuaded people to give up their long-held beliefs in other gods. There is some evidence that the old religion continued for a long time alongside the new one, and some aspects of it became incorporated in Christian writings, leading some to see the development of a distinctive 'Celtic Christianity' and a 'Celtic Church'. For example, Brigit, one of the most revered saints in medieval Ireland, is thought to be a Christianised version of the pagan Celtic goddess Brigit, and important saint's days often coincide with the major Celtic festivals such as Samain (Halloween) and Beltane (Mayday). Most scholars now reject the idea of a

On previous page
Currach
This reconstruction of a seventh-century currach was sailed from Ireland to Iona to celebrate the 1400th anniversary of Columba's death in AD 597.
KILMARTIN HOUSE TRUST/DAVID LYONS

'Celtic Church', believing that there were differences of practice between all the churches in the 'Celtic' areas, but that all regarded themselves as belonging to the standard Roman church of the continent.

There are many unanswered questions about early Christianity in the Gaelic areas, and controversies abound because religious questions became enmeshed with modern religious, nationalist and political viewpoints. The early Christian monk, Columba (in Gaelic *Colum Cille,* 'the dove of the church'), occupies a central place in many of these controversies. Was he a missionary, intent on converting the heathen, or was he retreating from the world, to a 'desert in the ocean'? Did he convert the Pictish king and set up monasteries in eastern Scotland? Had he committed some terrible crime that led to his exile from Ireland? Did he ordain and anoint the king of Dál Riata, Aedán mac Gabráin, two centuries before the practice was adopted on the continent? We cannot answer these questions here, but what is interesting is the way in which Columba's life has been interpreted by many different people to support their own view of the past. This process has been going on since at least the seventh century when Adomnán (Columba's successor as abbot of Iona) wrote his biography of Columba.

One factor which stands out above all others in the effects of Christianity was the introduction of writing, which was closely associated with Columba.

The power of writing

Living in a world where we are utterly dependent on the written word, in books, newspapers, road signs and computer screens, it is difficult for us to imagine what life was like in an oral society like early Dál Riata. All knowledge in these communities resided in the seers *(filid),* amongst whom were poets *(ollam),* judges and law-keepers *(brithem)* and lore-masters *(senchaid),* Their knowledge depended on their ability to memorise enormous bodies of information. Our distance from this type of society makes it easy to underestimate the impact and power of writing when such societies came into contact with literate people. When Martin Martin travelled to St Kilda in 1697, he was the first literate person to land on these wild and isolated islands. The islanders' reaction to writing illustrates the almost magical qualities of writing, and the power it gives those who can utilise it:

> *but above all, writing was the most astonishing to them: they cannot conceive how it is possible for any mortal to express the conceptions of his mind in such black characters upon white paper. I told them, that*

within the compass of two years or less, if they pleased, they might easily be taught to read and write, but they were not of the opinion that either of them could be obtained, at least by them, in an age.

Writing was brought to Dál Riata by the first Christian monks, some of the earliest being Columba and his twelve companions who settled on Iona in the 560s. The study of the Latin Bible, and the copying of its texts, was a major part of the spiritual duties of these monks, but it was the ways in which writing was used in the outer world which was so influential. Those who could read became the new *filid,* as only they could interpret what was written down, either in the Bible, or in secular documents. Priests and monks therefore came to be the guardians of the 'truth', which in the case of writing appeared to be unchangeable because it was written down.

In this climate, the books themselves came to be seen as objects of power, and began to be elaborately decorated both on the internal pages and on the leather covers. Adomnán describes how Columba spent much time writing, continuing up until the day of his death. The monks of Iona used books, supposedly written by Columba, to perform various miracles. One particular manuscript, known as the *Cathach* (Battler) of Columba, survives in Ireland, where it was treated as a precious relic, encased in a shrine and used as the battle-standard of the army of the O'Donells of County Donegal. Tradition states that the *Cathach* was written by Columba, and it may well have been, as it has been dated to around 600 on the form of the script. The *Cathach* is important, not just as the earliest surviving book written in Scotland, but because it shows the first steps towards the elaborate decoration which led within a hundred years to the great illustrated manuscripts such as the Book of Durrow.

Although there has been a great deal of debate in the past, many scholars now believe that two of the finest illustrated manuscripts, the Book of Durrow and the Book of Kells, were among many produced in Iona in the seventh and eighth centuries. These illuminated gospels are a striking indication of the wealth of resources which had been accumulated by monasteries since their modest beginnings in the sixth century. Apart from the human resources required to produce these works, estimated at one man-year for the more highly decorated books, the physical resources required were enormous. At least 185 calves had to be killed to produce the special sections of hide needed for the vellum pages of the Book of Kells. This would require a herd of at least 600 cattle to sustain the breeding population. The colouring materials used in the painted pages were rare and expensive, coming from places as far away as the Mediterranean (orpiment for yellow colours) and Afghanistan

Cathach of Columba

This manuscript is probably the oldest surviving book written in Scotland, dating from around AD 600. Tradition says Columba himself wrote the book. This work shows the first steps towards the illustrated manuscripts such as the Book of Kells in the use of coloured dots, small crosses, and an enlarged initial letter.

ROYAL IRISH ACADEMY, DUBLIN

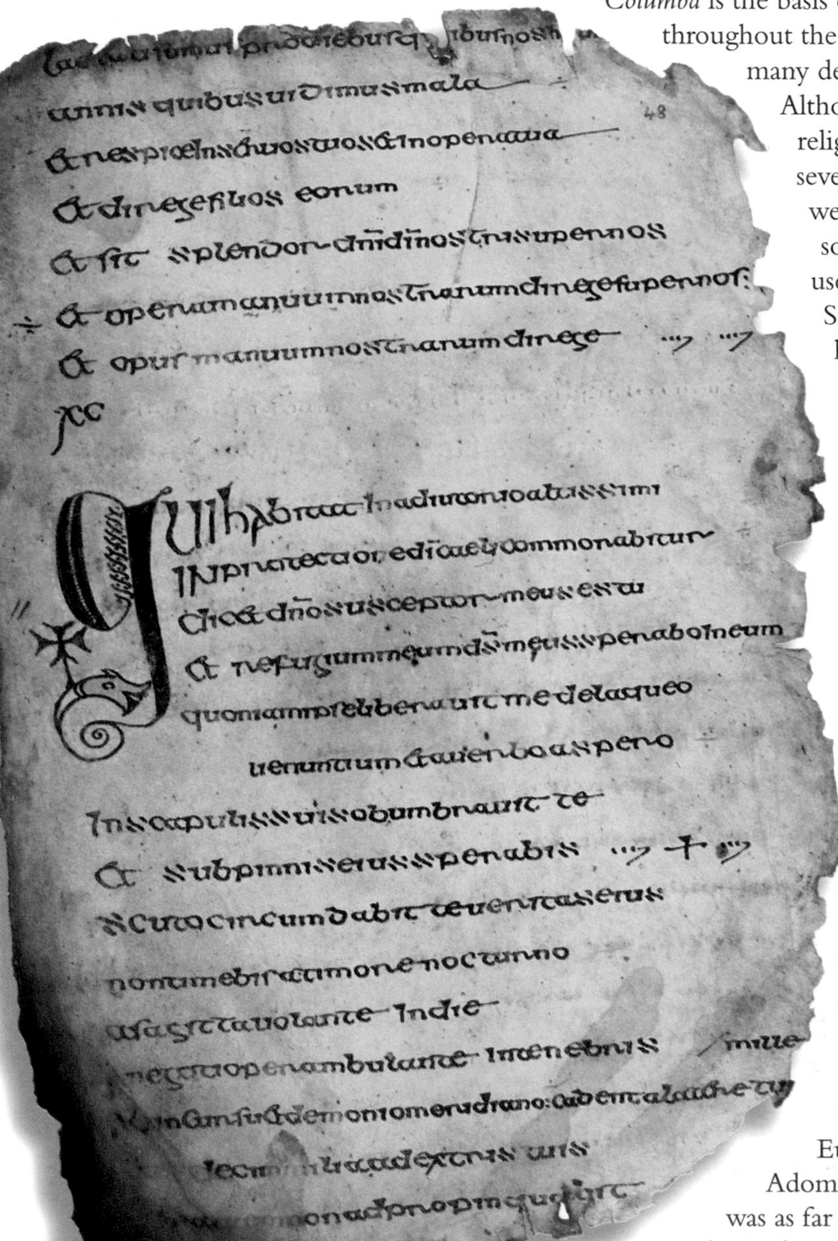

(lapis lazuli for blue). It is no wonder that the monasteries were prime targets of the Norse raiders in the ninth century, if they held such wealth.

Although the books of the gospel were important as powerful symbols, it was the newly composed, rather than copied, writings which had the greater impact on society. Several works which show how the Church was able to influence secular society were also products of Iona. Adomnán's *Life of Saint Columba* is the basis of the fame of Columba throughout the medieval world, and provides many details of daily life on Iona. Although it is outwardly a work of religious praise, Adomnán had several political messages which were put forward in a subtle and sophisticated manner. He tried to use Old Testament kings such as Solomon to provide a model of how the Church and king could support each other. As Columba's successor, he wanted to be in a position to ordain or anoint the new king at his inauguration, so he invented a story claiming that Columba ordained the Dalriadic king Aedán mac Gabráin, and chose him in preference to his brothers. *The Life of Saint Columba* was widely copied and read on the continent, and Adomnán's invented inauguration ritual may have been adopted by the Carolingian kings of France.

Adomnán's other writings were equally influential. His description of the holy places of Palestine, *De Locis Sanctis,* became the main guidebook to the Holy Land in early medieval Europe, despite the fact that Adomnán never went there and Iona was as far from Jerusalem as it was possible to be in the civilised world at this time. A collection of church laws, the *Collectio*

Adomnán writing

This illustration shows Adomnán in the abbot's cell on Torr an Aba writing his *Life of Saint Columba*, based oncontemporary drawings of scribes at work. Monks at Iona spent many hours of the day copying and illuminating religious texts as part of their monastic duties. Adomnán and others also composed many new works, including poetry, and made use of the extensive library which we know existed in the monastery. Adomnán is shown with the Celtic fashion of tonsure where the front half of the head is shaved, rather than the Roman where the top half is shaven. Adomnán supported the introduction of Roman practices, but was unable to persuade the monks at Iona to abandon their traditional ways over the tonsure and the method of calculating Easter.

DAVID HOGG

Canonum Hibernensis, is also now thought to have been compiled under Adomnán at Iona, and formed the basis of church law throughout much of Europe for hundreds of years. Adomnán was able to undertake the scholarship shown in these works using the extensive library which existed on Iona. The contents of this library, which can be reconstructed from passages quoted in

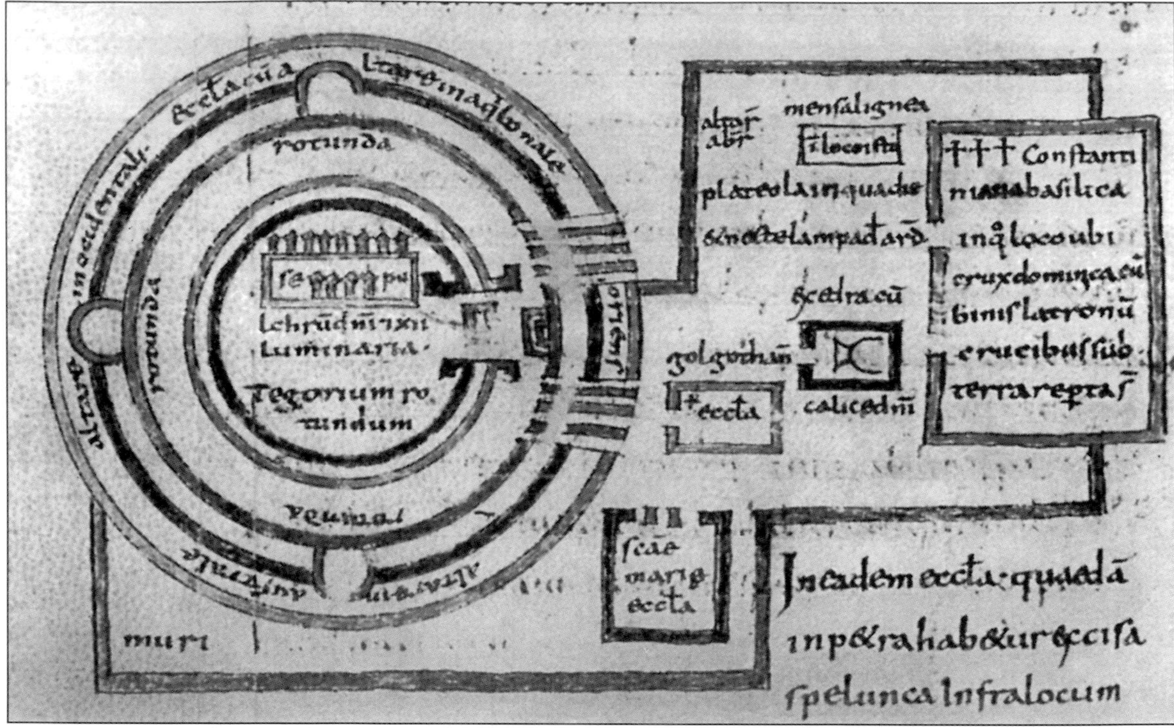

Church Plan
Adomnán's guide to the Holy Places contained this sketch of the Church of the Holy Sepulchre in Jerusalem, probably the oldest architectural drawing from Scotland. Adomnán based his account on information from a Gaulish bishop, Arculf, who had spent many months in Palestine, but with typical thoroughness he checked Arculf's story against other works in the Iona library to provide a balanced account which remained a standard work for many centuries.
ÖSTERREICHISCHE NATIONALBIBLIOTHEK, WIEN, COD. 458

works written on Iona, included all the major biblical texts and commentaries available at the time.

One final work of Adomnán's shows his political influence and his unique ability to innovate. In 697 he produced one of the earliest known attempts to assert an international declaration of human rights. His Law of Innocents, *Cáin Adomnáin,* tried to protect non-combatants (women, children and clerics) in time of war.

> *That women may not be killed by a man in any way, neither by slaughter or by any other death, not by poison, nor in water, nor in fire, nor by any beast, nor in a pit, nor by dogs, but shall die in their own lawful bed.*

Adomnán managed to get the law guaranteed by a list of over fifty Irish kings, the king of Dál Riata, and the king of the Picts.

The works of Adomnán make it clear why Iona had such a high reputation in early medieval times, and was one of the major

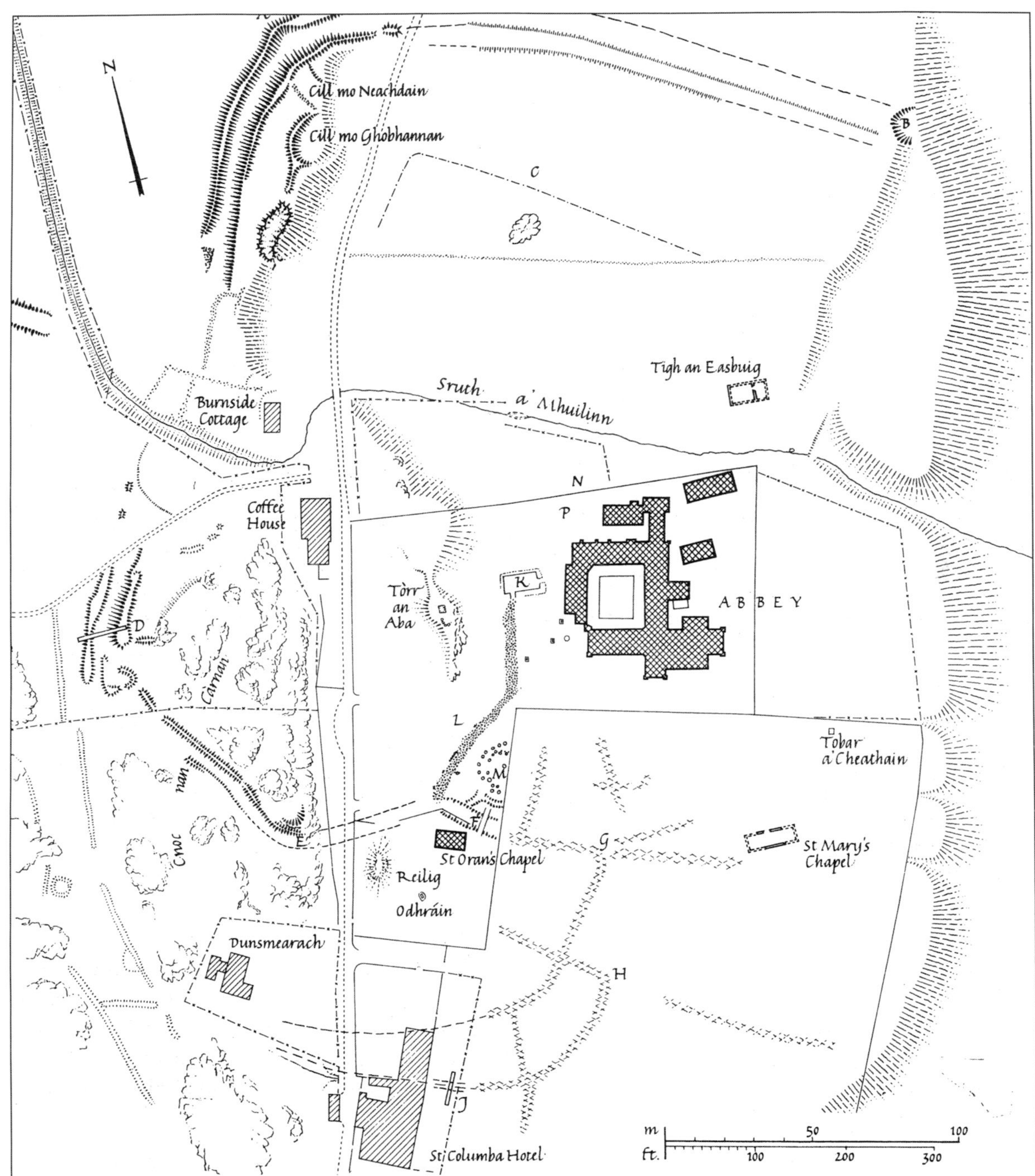

Iona

We know very little of the layout of the early monastery at Iona, despite numerous excavations. The most obvious feature is the monastic vallum or bank, which symbolised the separation of the monastery from the outside world. Unlike most other monasteries of the time it is not circular in plan. It may be of several dates, as some parts appear to be dated to the Iron Age, and other sections to the sixth century. In the ditch associated with the bank there were many wooden objects. The foundations of a hut on Tòrr an Aba have been interpreted as Columba's cell. A large structure outlined by double lines of posts (M) has recently been interpreted as a pigsty. The positions of some of the high crosses may be original, though they may have stood at the boundaries of the enclosure. The Reilig Odhráin is the traditional burial place of kings, and may be the site of the monastic graveyard.

St Martin's Cross

This cross from Iona is perhaps the earliest. It shows Biblical scenes, in this case David with the musicians, set amongst interlaced decoration copied from metalwork and illustrated manuscripts.

RCAHMS: CROWN COPYRIGHT

centres of learning in Europe despite its position on the fringes of the civilised world.

Writing also transformed the world outside the Church. We have already seen that in the seventh century the *Senchus Fer nAlban* was a survey of the population of Argyll, used by the kings of Dál Riata to assess the amount of tribute and war-muster from each area. Such a census was impossible without writing, and represents the beginnings of state bureaucracy, our modern-day income tax forms included! This listing of his subjects enabled the king to change the way he ruled because tribute could be collected directly rather than through his nobles. The *Senchus* was one of the earliest census documents in Europe. In England the first attempt to survey the population in this detail was the Domesday Book in the 1080s.

Inscribed Stone
This little pebble from old excavations at Dunadd has the letters 'Inomine' inscribed on it, possibly as a talisman or a trial piece. The Latin word represents the opening two words of a blessing, and show the presence of a literate person at the royal site.
NATIONAL MUSEUMS OF SCOTLAND

The other major feature of the *Senchus* is the lists giving genealogies of the kings and nobles. Once these were written down it was easy for later kings to alter them to suit their own purposes. Modern historians have shown that the manipulation of king-lists and genealogies took place throughout this period, and most early lists are now known to be untrustworthy. Although oral accounts of ancestors can also be altered to suit differing conditions, the written word is much more powerful as a record of the past, and until recent times these early traditions were taken at face value. We do not know who wrote the *Senchus,* but we can suspect it was a cleric or someone trained in a monastery. A small stone with a scratched Latin word found at the royal site of Dunadd might be a relict of a cleric who recorded information for the king. This little stone may be the only archaeological remnant of a process which was leading to the eventual replacement of an oral culture by one based on the written word.

The power of images

The Church had to be able to present its message to an illiterate population. Priests would preach, often in the open air in front of a cross, and perhaps hold or read from a sacred book carried round in a leather satchel. It could be difficult for a large congregation to see a small image on a page, so eventually larger

permanent images were carved on the crosses. The sermons could then be multimedia experiences where the spoken word was reinforced with images. This led to the development of one of the outstanding achievements of the Gaelic world, the carved High Crosses, with their distinctive ring-head, interlaced decoration and biblical scenes. There are strong reasons for believing these crosses were invented in Iona, perhaps from a wooden prototype, as one of the earliest has the arms of the cross formed from separate pieces of stone fitted together with mortise and tenon joints just like wooden constructions. The ring was then added to support the weight of the arms after an early cross collapsed. At first the ring was separate, but later the masons realised it was easier to carve the whole ring-head from one piece of stone. The ring-headed crosses spread throughout Dál Riata and Ireland and are now seen as typically 'Celtic'. In the fourteenth and fifteenth centuries there was a revival of this form of cross in the Highlands and Islands, and then again in the nineteenth century with the rise of 'Highland mania' under the influence of Sir Walter Scott. Sadly debased examples are still being produced today and can be found in gift shops and graveyards throughout Britain.

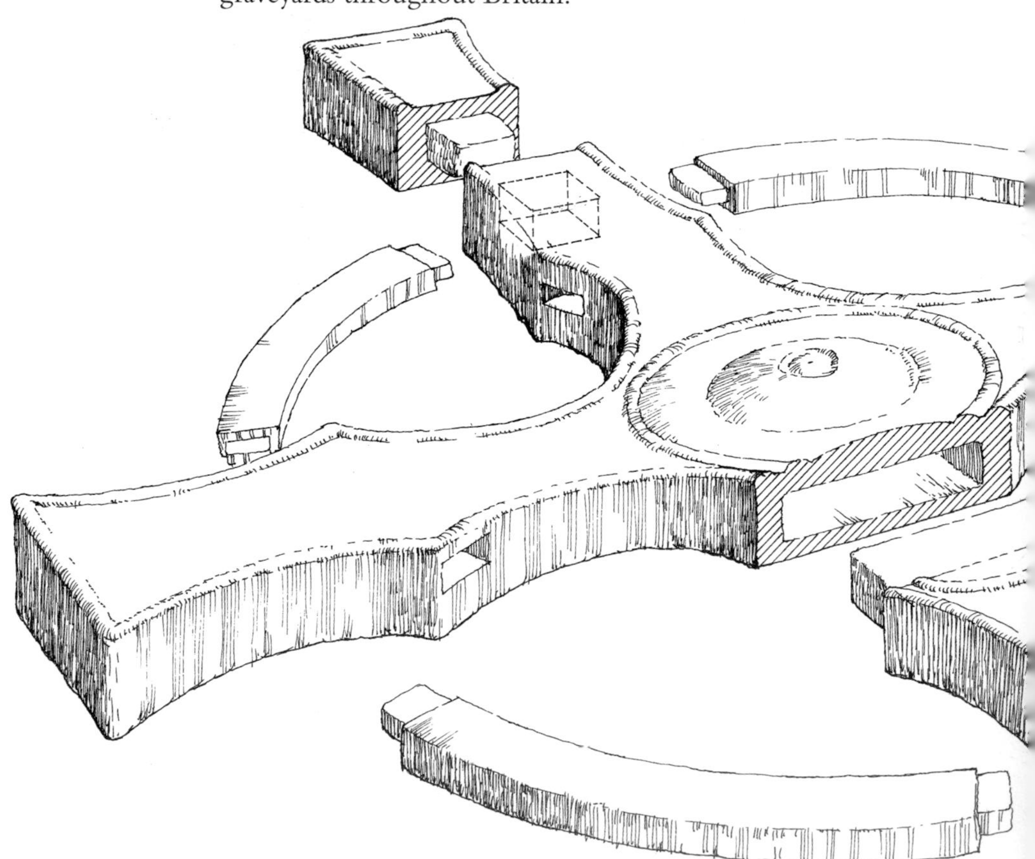

The Iona crosses brought together a fusion of other crafts alongside those of the mason and sculptor. The elaborate bosses on some crosses come from metalworking techniques, sometimes representing rivet-heads; the interlace decoration and figures come from illuminated manuscripts; and the structures come from carpentry techniques. It was characteristic of Dál Riata at this period that an entirely new type of object was created by combining elements from different areas.

The figures on the crosses represent key scenes from the Bible, such as Daniel in the lion's den, the nativity, and David with his musicians. As well as illustrating sermons, they could be an aid to contemplation. Modern analysis has shown that many of the scenes can have several layers of meaning so that the same scene could be used to illustrate different points of scripture in relation to everyday life. The interlace and knotwork covering many of the crosses was not purely decorative. The interlaced animals, particularly snakes, may have had a protective influence, guarding the cross against evil influence. Overall there is no doubt that the crosses of Dál Riata represent some of the most important works of sculpture in medieval Europe.

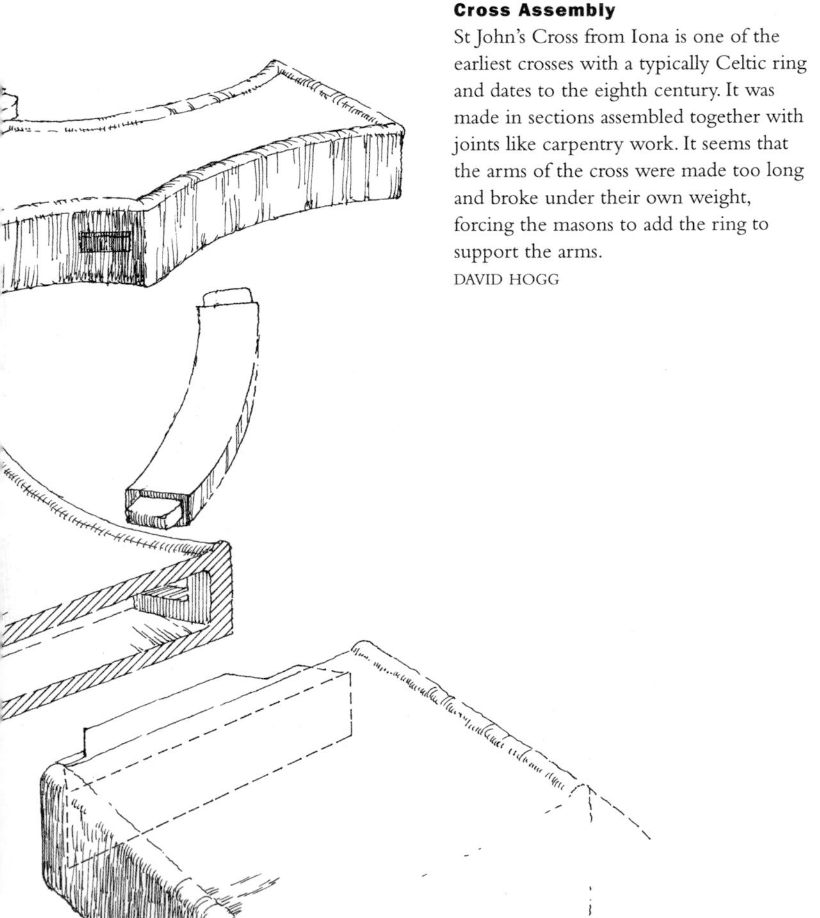

Cross Assembly
St John's Cross from Iona is one of the earliest crosses with a typically Celtic ring and dates to the eighth century. It was made in sections assembled together with joints like carpentry work. It seems that the arms of the cross were made too long and broke under their own weight, forcing the masons to add the ring to support the arms.
DAVID HOGG

Medieval Map

This map shows how the world would have looked from Iona in the seventh century. It is based on the places and journeys mentioned by Adomnán and in the annals.

DAVID HOGG

On the Edge of the World?

While the kingdom of Dál Riata was forming in western Scotland, Europe was going through similar profound changes. After the collapse of the western Roman Empire, the main power centre gradually shifted from the Mediterranean to France with the rise of the Carolingian Holy Roman Empire. World maps of these times show that western Scotland was on the edge of the known world: nothing was known of the areas to the west and north. This view surfaces again and again in the history of the Highland areas, from the viewpoint variously of Europeans, English and Scottish Lowlanders. For much of the later middle ages, the area was under the control of the Norse (outwith the general political developments in Scotland), or under the semi-independent Lords of the Isles. Even today, the 'Celtic Fringe' is used as a term of dismissal about the western areas of Britain, indicating that they were on the periphery of civilisation. It is difficult to counter this general impression, and show that in the early middle ages Dál Riata was at the forefront of political, artistic and religious innovation. In this chapter we will look at some of the archaeological evidence which shows that the Dalriadans had contacts with many other regions and were by no means cut off on the periphery of Europe. In fact, as we shall see, Dál Riata was more of a crossroads than a backwater.

Continental Pottery
This type of pottery was produced in western France, and used as containers for dyestuffs and other luxury commodities. This almost complete vessel comes from Loch Glashan crannog.
GLASGOW MUSEUMS AND ART GALLERIES

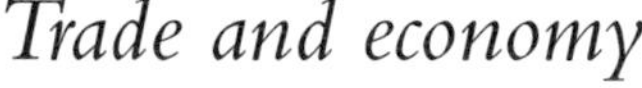

Trade and economy

In recent years archaeologists have found evidence that Dál Riata was part of a trading network which linked France with western Britain and Ireland in the late sixth and seventh centuries. A trail of sites which have remains of continental pottery and glass vessels show that the sailing routes reached up the Irish Sea as far

Traders

Merchants from western France brought many luxury goods to Dál Riata. They probably landed at an island in Crinan Harbour where they exchanged wine, salt, dyestuffs and exotic spices for local goods and slaves.
DAVID HOGG

north as Argyll. In fact, Dunadd has the largest quantity of continental pottery of any site in Britain, and Whithorn in Galloway has the largest quantity of glass vessels. The evidence raises a whole series of questions: what was being traded, who were the traders, who was receiving goods and what were they using them for, and why did this trade start much earlier in Scotland than in Anglo-Saxon England? We know the answers to some of these through scientific analysis, but others have to be more conjectural.

Pottery was not made or used in Dál Riata, because people preferred wooden, metal and leather vessels. The pottery which came from the continent was used as containers to bring in a variety of luxuries not obtainable in Britain. Scientific analysis of stains on the insides of pots from Dunadd has shown that some were used for transporting red or purple dyestuffs made from the plant Dyer's madder. This plant is not native to western Europe, but was grown on royal estates in France. Other exotic plant seeds, including coriander and dill, have been found in waterlogged deposits along with continental pottery. These spices and herbs were also grown in France, so it is likely that a whole

variety of other commodities, such as nuts, dates and sweetmeats, mentioned in documents, were brought in along with the pottery. These luxury goods were not the main commodity of trade as they took up little cargo space. Most of the hold of each trading ship was filled with wine barrels or containers of salt. Both of these came from western France, but leave no trace in the archaeological record. The wine could have been drunk from the conical glass beakers found on many sites. Because the pottery and glass came from western France, we think that French traders were carrying out the trade. Adomnán's *Life of Saint Columba* even mentions Gaulish traders coming to the 'chief place of the region', probably to Dunadd. But who were they trading with? It used to be thought it was the Church, who needed wine for the celebration of the Eucharist, but the largest quantities of imports are on secular royal sites and very little is found on religious sites.

Trade Routes
Dál Riata's trading connections were widespread, using the west coast sea-routes to bring exotic goods from all over Britain and the continent.
HISTORIC SCOTLAND/ROB BURNS

The picture which emerges from this new evidence is at odds with the traditional view of barbarism and backwardness on the 'Celtic Fringe'. Here we have Dalriadan kings entertaining their nobles and guests with fine French wines, drunk from expensive, fragile decorated glasses, eating spice-laden food and passing round dainty tit-bits from the sun-drenched Mediterranean lands. Equivalent imports did not reach the courts of most of England until a century later.

Whatever was being traded for these goods is not visible archaeologically: no Dalriadan objects are known from the area of the French traders. Slaves were probably the main export, though natural resources like furs, eiderdown and leather goods are other possibilities. We have seen how leather goods were produced at Loch Glashan, and there is a reference to Irish

leather goods sold at the mouth of the River Loire in the eighth century. Although large quantities of imports come from royal sites such as Dunadd, Dunollie, Dumbarton and Clogher in Tyrone, there are many smaller sites in Dál Riata which had a few imports. These are sites such as Ardifuir and Loch Glashan close to Dunadd, or Kildalloig Dun in Kintyre. These small amounts represent gifts of luxuries from the king to his nobles which helped to cement social relations. Other goods probably came in which were of use to the Church. A piece of the mineral orpiment, which must have come from the Mediterranean, came from Dunadd. This was used to produce the bright yellow colour seen in illustrated manuscripts such as the Book of Durrow. The king gave materials like these to the abbot of Iona in return for favours such as the right to be buried on Iona, or the loan of monks to help produce documents such as the *Senchus*. The one imported pot found on Iona shows how these luxuries may have been carried to Iona from Dunadd. By controlling the inflow of these luxuries the king was able to enhance his standing with his nobles and with the Church. The Church in return asked favours of the king. The magnificent stone crosses of Iona were carved out of rock which comes from Doide, Loch Sween. The king must have given permission for the monks to quarry this rock. Incidentally, the seamanship required to bring these huge slabs of rock, up to 4.5 metres long and weighing several tonnes, in a lightweight currach across 80km of open sea, was of the highest quality.

Many other exotic goods found at Dunadd were brought in this trading system. Analysis of molten metal droplets show that bars of native tin were brought from Cornwall. A tessera cube from a mosaic is made of blue glass with a thin film of gold leaf sandwiched within it. These are of Mediterranean origin, where they were used to create the golden mosaic wall panels in the churches of Ravenna and Byzantium. The cube may have been a

Exotic Pigment
Minerals such as this orpiment found at Dunadd were brought enormous distances to provide the colours for illuminated manuscripts. This mineral from the Mediterranean was used to produce the yellow colour in the Book of Kells.
EWAN CAMPBELL

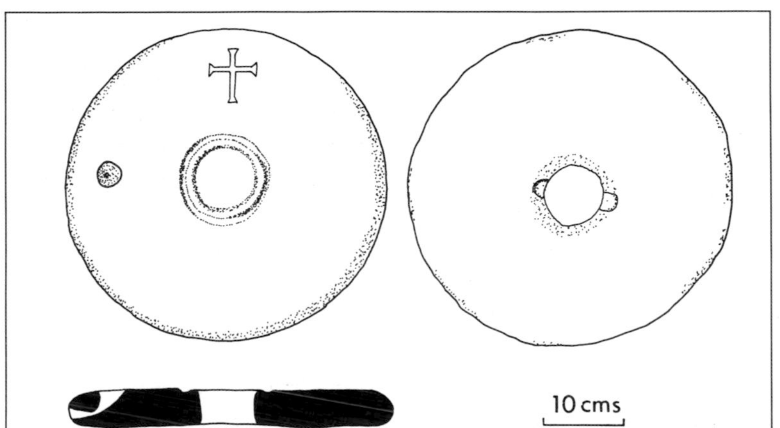

Cross-marked Quern
This corn-grinding quern from Dunadd was special because it was of an unusual rock type, and had a neat cross incised on it. The quern may have been a gift from the monks of Iona, or it may have been blessed for royal use.
RCAHMS: CROWN COPYRIGHT

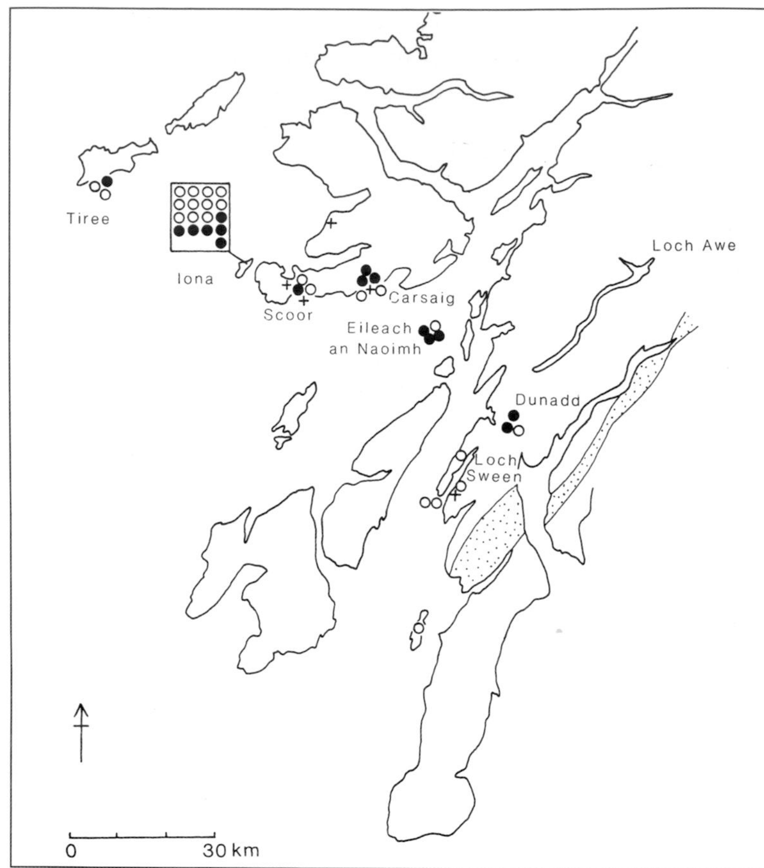

Distribution Map
This map shows the distribution of inscribed crosses like the one on the quern from Dunadd. There are clear links between Iona and Dunadd.
EWAN CAMPBELL

keepsake brought back by a pilgrim, but these glass cubes were also melted down for bead-making. From Anglo-Saxon England came gold and garnet jewellery, and silver buckles. More mundane materials are the pieces of oil-shale from the Lowland coal fields which were used to make bracelets.

The overall picture is of a sophisticated trading network, integrating the exploitation of local resources with the import and redistribution of commodities from all over western Europe. The emphasis in Dalriadic society on the use of ships and on maritime knowledge was crucial to this trading system. As the historical documents of the period are almost completely silent about such trade, its discovery is one of the major contributions of archaeology to changing our perceptions of Dál Riata.

Artistic interaction: the melting pot of styles

We have already seen that there is plenty of archaeological and historical evidence for contacts between Dál Riata and other regions, ranging from Ireland to Northumbria, Cornwall to Dumbarton, and Pictland to France. These contacts are also expressed in the art styles of the sculpture, metalwork and manuscripts. The patterns of interlaced animal ornament, and

complex spirals and knotwork which is so characteristic of this period arose from a fusion of elements from Anglo-Saxon, Irish and Pictish art. By the eighth century the different elements were integrated into one style, the Insular style. Art historians have long argued about where the important works of art of the period were made. When an Englishman suggested that the Book of Kells was made in Northumbria, Irish historians were outraged, seeing it as a form of cultural colonialism with the English trying to steal their Irish birthright. In recent years, archaeology has helped to inform some of these heated debates, and in particular the excavations at Dunadd have shown that Dál Riata was one of the areas where this fusion of styles was taking place.

At Dunadd, there were deposits full of debris from a metalworking workshop. Hundreds of discarded fragments of crucibles, moulds for brooches, metal droplets, tools and unfinished items were found. It was not just raw materials like the tin from Cornwall which came from distant sources. A tiny setting of deep red garnet surrounded by twisted gold filigree wires belonged to a piece of Anglo-Saxon jewellery of the highest quality, matched only by items in the great royal treasure from the Sutton Hoo ship-burial. One mould was of a buckle of Anglo-Saxon type, with silver still adhering to it. Buckles are not a Celtic item of dress, so this one was made by a Saxon metalworker working at Dunadd. But local craft workers were also at work here, as shown by the numerous moulds for brooches of western types. Another exotic item is a round enamelled disc with Celtic spirals and triskeles of a type often found on bowls in Saxon graves, but believed to have been made in Pictland. There is also a small triangular bronze plaque stamped with animal ornament similar to that in the Book of Durrow. So Dunadd was a site where all the elements which made up the Insular style – Pictish, Saxon and Irish – were in one place. This is not surprising, as there is historical evidence for contacts between Northumbria, Pictland and the British of Dumbarton. We know that Anglian princes and their retinues from Northumbria were in exile at the court of Dál Riata throughout the seventh century, Columba visited the Pictish king Bridei, probably on a diplomatic mission, Adomnán visited Aldfrith the Anglian king, and another Iona monk was sent on a mission to the king of the Britons at Dumbarton. Unlike manuscripts or brooches, which can be carried around the country so we can never be sure where they were made, the archaeological evidence is important because it shows where items were actually being made.

Another important find was several fragments of a very large brooch which was of a type like the famous Hunterston and Tara

Enamelled Disc
A recent find from Dunadd.
HOWARD MASON

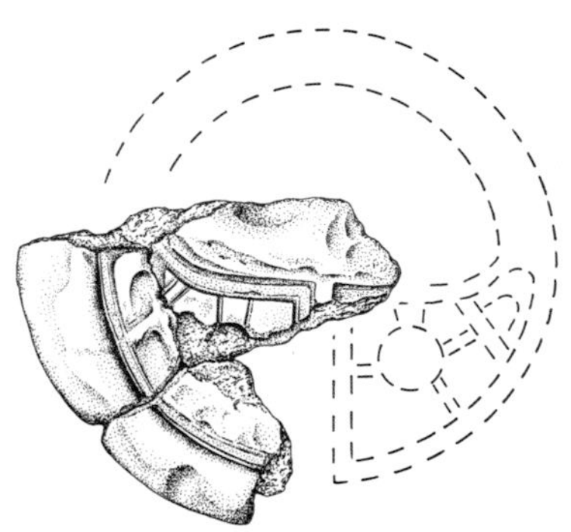

Brooch Mould
These recently found mould fragments from Dunadd were used to cast a large brooch with panelled decoration. The panels would have been infilled with gold filigree designs.
EWAN CAMPBELL, HOWARD MASON

Hunterston Brooch (right)
The Hunterston brooch is one of the outstanding achievements of Late Celtic metalworking. Although a typically Celtic type, the eagle heads are an Anglo-Saxon element. It has been suggested that the central cross-shaped panel concealed a small holy relic.
NATIONAL MUSEUMS OF SCOTLAND

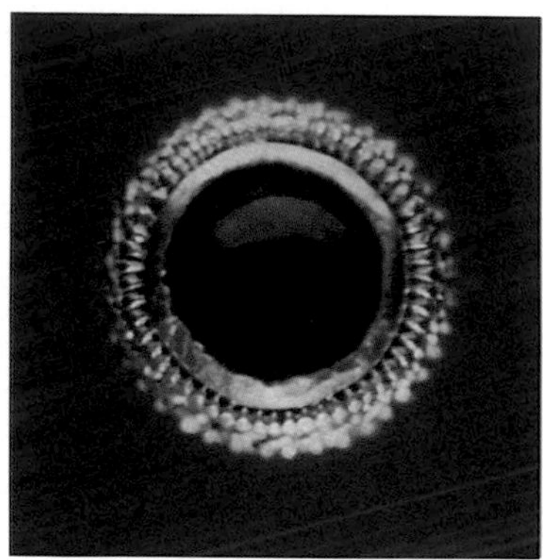

Jewellery Setting (above)
This tiny gold and garnet setting, found in the metalworking workshop at Dunadd, has been ripped from an Anglo-Saxon piece of jewellery, probably for recycling. The quality of the workmanship is outstanding, and the original jewellery may have belonged to an Anglo-Saxon prince.
CARDIFF UNIVERSITY

brooches, which are amongst the outstanding examples of metalwork of any period. Until this find it was thought that these originated in Ireland, but it now seems that Dál Riata could also have produced similar items. We have seen how these brooches were worn as a sign of a person's rank in society. Between the sixth and eighth centuries brooches became larger and much more elaborate, perhaps showing that wealth was increasing amongst the nobles, or that there was increasing distance between different classes of society. These were changes which continued in the later middle ages.

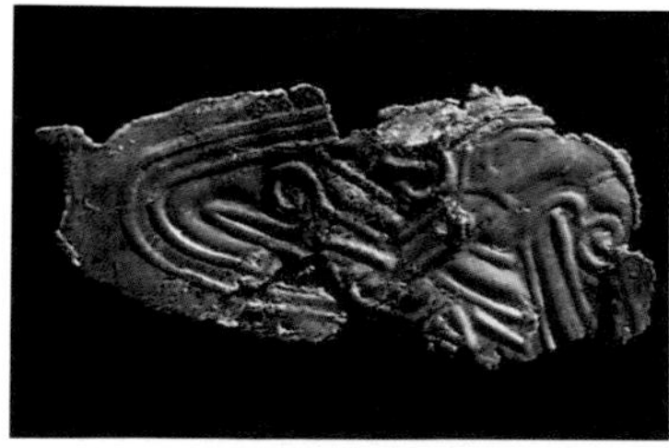

Decorated Foil (above)
This thin bronze foil from Dunadd has been stamped with animal ornament. The animal design shows a mixture of Anglo-Saxon and Celtic design, and has similarities to the beasts in the Book of Durrow.
CARDIFF UNIVERSITY

Book of Durrow (Opposite Page)
The ornament of the great illuminated manuscripts shows a mixture of influences from Pictish, Anglo-Saxon and Irish art styles. Dál Riata was a key place where these influences came into contact with each other. The Book of Durrow was probably made in Iona in the later seventh century.
THE BOARD OF TRINITY COLLEGE DUBLIN

Silver Brooches
These bird-headed silver brooches are exact replicas of types found in moulds at Dunadd. They date to the seventh century, and are based on an Anglo-Saxon design, adapted to the Celtic fashion of brooch fastening.
KILMARTIN HOUSE TRUST/DAVID LYONS

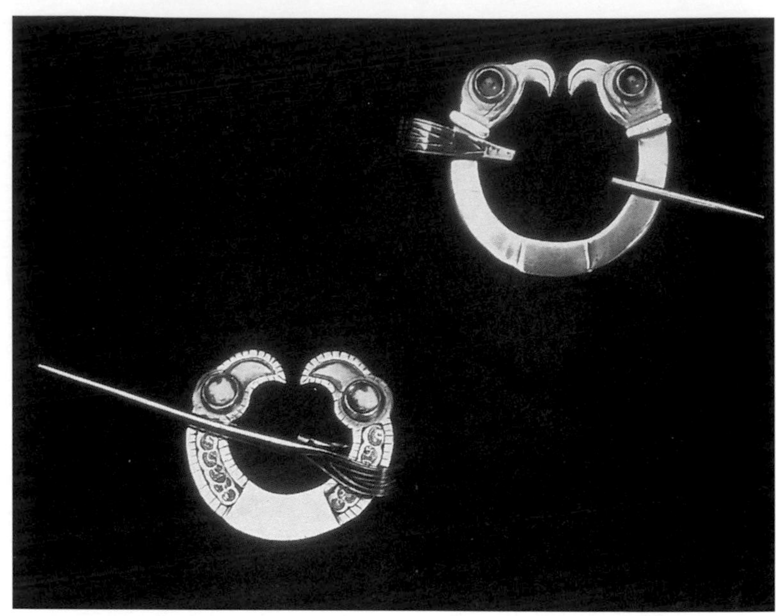

Politics and war

Archaeological evidence has shown us that Dál Riata was in no way an area isolated from the rest of Britain and Europe. Historical accounts support this picture, and can add names of individuals, places and events to give a more human scale to the account. Although reliable references are very sparse, mainly relating to battles, the deaths of kings, princes and abbots, and genealogies of royalty, some historians have used them to construct a picture of the general political development of Dál Riata. This written material is exceptionally difficult to untangle because of layers of additions, translations and mistaken copying which have built up over the centuries of transmission. Even after generations of study, historians cannot agree on such a basic thing as a definitive list of the kings of Dál Riata and their dates of rule. There are also gaps in the evidence, which mainly relates to the seventh and eighth centuries. While we should be grateful to history for providing the human detail in the story, it is sometimes too easy to accept what is said by historians because they appear to be speaking about real people. Some modern historians of the period would reject the possibility of constructing a meaningful story from these meagre sources.

Despite these problems some points seem to be generally accepted. For most of the time there was an overking of Dál Riata, who was chosen from one of the two leading peoples, the Cenél Loairn and the Cenél nGabráin. The kingship originally belonged to the Cenél nGabráin of Kintyre, but in the eighth century it passed to the Cenél Loairn whose stronghold was the

fort of Dunollie just outside Oban. There were conflicts between the different kindreds, perhaps over the succession, and sub-kings of the regions may have occasionally become powerful enough to challenge the over-king, but on the whole the overkingship was a stable institution. This is unusual at this period, compared with the situation in Ireland or England where overkingship fluctuated between powerful individual kings with little stability of

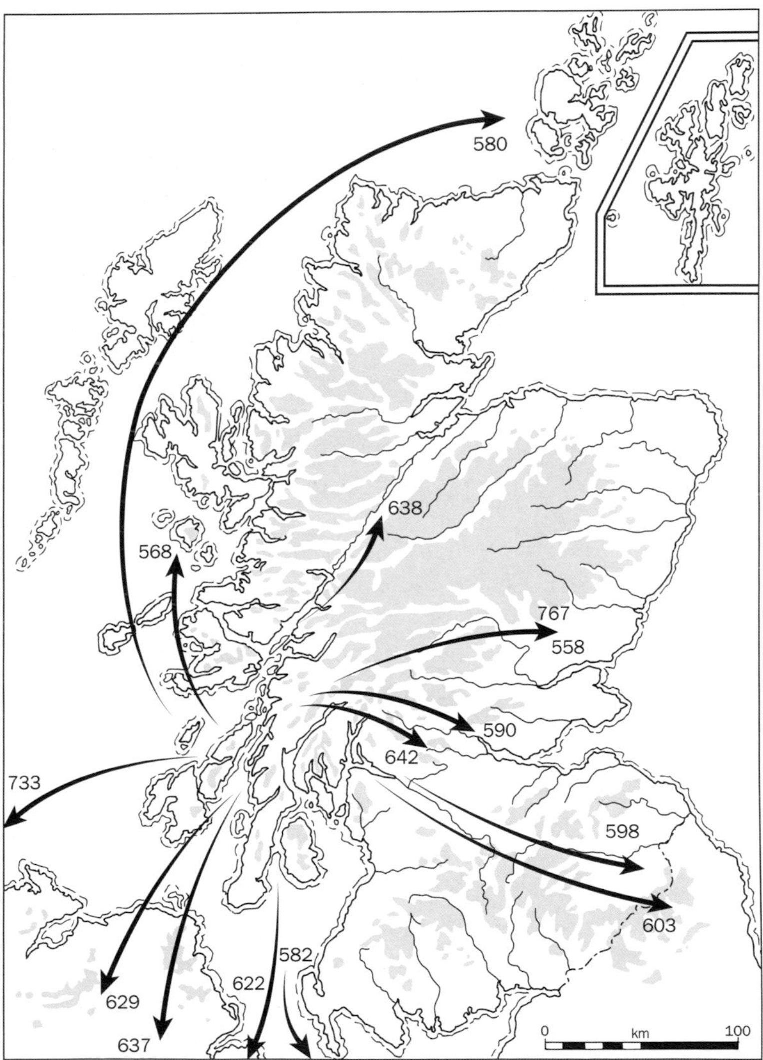

Battle Campaigns
Dál Riata fought battle campaigns throughout northern Britain and Ireland, by land and sea. The map shows the dates of all the recorded battles which are mentioned in contemporary sources. During the same period there are only two records of armies invading Dál Riata.
HISTORIC SCOTLAND/ROB BURNS

succession. The rivalry between the two major peoples of Dál Riata seems to have continued after the takeover of Pictland, and led to the rewriting of the origin legends in the tenth century to emphasise the position of the descendants of the Cenél nGabráin

A few kings stand out from the number of references to their activities. The first is Aedán mac Gabráin, who reigned from about AD 574 to AD 608. Aedán's main fort was probably Dunadd, and he was well-known to Columba, even if Adomnan's

Sea Battle

The Irish annals record a naval battle between two kindreds of Dál Riata in AD 719. Both curraghs and wooden boats were probably involved and there could have been up to a hundred boats on each side.

DAVID HOGG

story of Columba ordaining Aedán was a later invention. Aedán is recorded as hosting many expeditions, most of which seem to have been successful. The range of Aedán's battles illustrates how mobile the Dalriadan forces were, fighting in Orkney, Ireland, the Isle of Man and the Scottish Borders. He was finally defeated by the Northumbrians in 603 as he tried to halt their advance into southern Scotland. Why most of these battles, and those of other kings, took place is not known. Some may have been raids to gain wealth such as slaves, cattle or precious goods. Others may have been defensive reactions to the expansion of other kingdoms, or attempts to force neighbours into submission and exact tribute. Most of the time there does not seem to have been a wish by Dál Riata to expand into other areas. Dál Riata generally seems to have been friendly with the neighbouring British kingdoms, but on the other hand there was often conflict with the Picts to the east. No other king of Dál Riata fought so

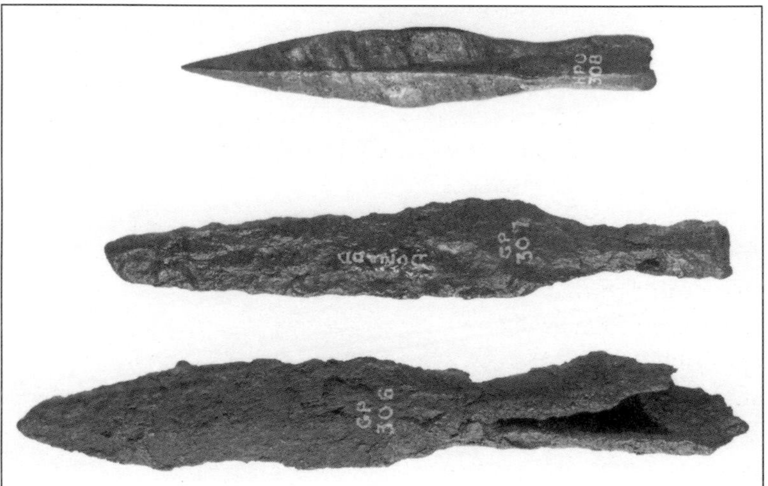

Weapons
Two spearheads and an arrowhead from among the large collection of weapons found at Dunadd.
NATIONAL MUSEUMS OF SCOTLAND

widely outside his territory as Aedán. The conventional view is that Dál Riata came under the domination of the Northumbrians and later Picts for much of the seventh and eighth centuries, though in fact there is little historical evidence to support this view.

We can say a little about how this warfare was conducted. The *Senchus* allows us to estimate that a maximum of about 2000 fighting men were available in the seventh century. This is a considerable force, similar in size to a Roman legion, but small in comparison to the tens of thousands suggested for some Anglo-Saxon kingdoms at this period. The Dalriadans would have travelled mainly by boat, either currachs or wooden ships. The currachs may have been more suitable for raiding parties, with wooden ships being used for carrying stores. As we have seen, the earliest recorded naval battle took place in western

Political alliances

Warfare and trade were not the only means of contact between Dál Riata and other kingdoms. Marriage alliances between royal families were common. King Aedán may have married both British and Pictish princesses, and may have married one of his daughters to an Irish king. There are many other accounts of intermarriages between Pictish, Saxon, British and Gaelic royalty, although not all can be taken at face value as the genealogies were often manipulated to try to bolster claims to other kingdoms. We also hear of royal exiles, such as the Northumbrian princes, Oswald and Oswiu, who lived in exile in Dál Riata in the early seventh century. This may help to explain the Saxon metalwork found at Dunadd as these princes probably included metalworkers in their retinues, and were likely to have been guests of the king at Dunadd. Diplomatic contact between kings was essential, and it seems that the Church played a part in this. Columba's visit to King Bridei, and his presence at the Convention of Druim Cett, were probably political acts. Adomnán intervened with the Northumbrian king to gain the release of hostages, and, most famously, managed to get more than fifty kings to agree to his Law of the Innocents. What we know must be a fraction of the contacts which took place, and shows again how sea travel and control of the sea was an essential and central part of life in Dál Riata.

Scotland, but we do not know how such a battle would have been fought. The army could also undertake overland marches, reaching as far as the Southern Uplands in the battle of the place known as *Degsastan* in 603.

Spears and bows were probably the main weapons, with round shields for defence. Only aristocrats would have been able to afford swords. Crossbows were used, and some crossbow bolts have been found at Dunadd and Dunollie, but they were probably uncommon. Most set battles were between forces fighting on foot, with hand-to-hand combat. This is the type of semi-ritualised conflict glorified in the heroic poetry of the time, such as the British *Gododdin,* or the Saxon *Beowulf.* The Irish annals also record many instances of forts being besieged, destroyed or burnt. In Argyll, forts were attacked at least ten times in some fifty years from 683 to 736. Hillforts were clearly places of military strength even though, as at Dunadd, they may have had other important functions. There are no references to Dalriadan forts being attacked after the 740s, but this is due to a gap in the recording. Archaeological evidence shows that forts continued to be occupied, and presumably attacked, but the next conflicts we hear about in Dál Riata start in 794 with the first Viking raid on Scotland. The Vikings operated under different 'rules of engagement', and had little wish to lay siege to forts or engage in set battles. This may partly account for the outrage caused by their attacks on rich monasteries and churches. Talk of Vikings brings us to the end of our period, however, and marks the start of an era when Dál Riata ceased to exist in its own right.

Epilogue: the Flight to the East

By the middle of the ninth century the Dalriadan kings had extended their control over Pictland in eastern Scotland. From this time on, the homeland of Argyll slips into obscurity, later re-emerging as a border area between the influence of the Scottish kings and the Lords of the Isles. Most of the artistic achievements described in this book go into decline. There are no manuscripts

Early Christian Bell and Shrine
Bells, books and croziers belonging to early Celtic holy men were revered as relics and kept in specially constructed shrines. This seventh to ninth-century bell, and its later medieval shrine, were discovered in the nineteenth century at Kilmichael Glassary, only 2km from Dunadd. Many such relics had hereditary keepers called *tóiseach deòireach* in Gaelic, dewar in Scots. The MacLachlans of Dunadd are recorded as *tóiseach deòireach* up until the seventeenth century and were probably the last vestige of Dalriadan royal authority left in Argyll after the kings moved to the east in the ninth century.
NATIONAL MUSEUMS OF SCOTLAND

to match the Book of Kells, the metalwork becomes plainer and more crudely decorated, and the stone crosses less elaborate. The pattern and types of settlement change for the first time for a thousand years, away from hilltop duns to unenclosed farmsteads and clachans, and the royal forts are deserted. New political and religious power centres are set up: Dunadd is replaced by Scone,

Iona by St Andrews and Dunkeld. Pictish is replaced by Gaelic. Why all these changes took place is one of the most interesting questions of Scottish history, and is properly discussed in other books in this series. A programme of archaeological research is underway to try to understand exactly when the changes occurred, and what environmental, social and economic factors may have been involved. Without these answers we have only political explanations. I have tried to show in this book how the sea was the key to the success of Dál Riata, but it may also have contributed to its decline. The advent of the Norse may have exposed the Dalriadans to a sea-borne people with better ships than their own. The coastal location of settlement in Dál Riata may have made it particularly vulnerable to Viking raids, leading to a move of the nobility to the east. However, although there were extensive Norse settlements in the Northern and Western Isles, there is no evidence for any settlement in mainland Argyll, the heartland of Dál Riata, and it may be that the Dalriadan army and navy managed to hold off the Norse.

The kingdom of Dál Riata flourished for a brief few centuries, but the legacy of that period is profound. I have tried to show how Dál Riata was not an obscure, peripheral place, but held an important place in the artistic, intellectual and political life of north-western Europe. Some of the artistic achievements, such as the Book of Kells and the Iona stone crosses, are among the world's great works of art. Adomnán's Law of the Innocents, the precursor of human rights legislation, was the product of intellectual study combined with spiritual feeling. On a more mundane level, the bureaucratic organisation implied by the *Senchus* may have contributed to the early development of the unified Scottish state, one of the earliest in Europe. These achievements were the result of a readiness by the Dalriadans to accept and integrate elements of other cultures, allied to a strong emphasis on learning and artistic endeavour. If we wish to learn anything from the past, perhaps the lesson which Dál Riata provides for modern Scotland is that it is perfectly possible for a small and outlying region of Europe to make important contributions to the wider community of nations.

Replicas of early Christian bells
KILMARTIN HOUSE TRUST/DAVID LYONS

Sites around Western Scotland

Remains of the early medieval period are found in many areas of western Scotland, but they tend to be of restricted types. The most obvious are the stone-walled duns and forts which crown many crags and hilltops. However, few of these have been excavated and many could be of prehistoric date. The most visible monuments are the carved stone crosses of Christian churches, monasteries and burial grounds. Despite the wealth of documentary evidence for these early Christian centres, in this area there are almost no remains of buildings from before the twelfth century surviving above ground. Many small ruined stone chapels are found, either on their own or associated with deserted settlements, but again very few have been excavated. Crannogs can be seen as small islands in many lochs, but there is little else to see and most are inaccessible except by boat.

A number of the sites listed here are open to the public by Historic Scotland (HS) or by other agencies (P), but others are in private ownership and may need the permission of the land-owner to visit. Ordnance Survey Grid references are given for all the sites.

Bute

St Blane's Church, Kingarth (P). The Firth of Clyde. There are the remains of a stone enclosure wall, a unique circular cell, and many small stone crosses marking graves. Early excavations produced many slates with trial lettering and interlace design, of the seventh to eighth centuries. A steep walk from the signposted car park.
NS 094534

Inner Hebrides

Iona (P). The island is reached by ferry from Fionnophort on Mull, where there is a new visitor centre. There are a large number of areas of interest for the early medieval period, all well signposted, but perhaps the most important feature of the island to experience is its unique atmosphere and setting.

The monastic vallum (enclosing bank) is the only visible sign of the early monastery. Excavations of the ditch have provided evidence of wood and leather working, and elsewhere faint traces of wooden buildings within the enclosure.

The most spectacular monuments are the high crosses, the most complete being St Martin's Cross of the eighth century. Four of the high crosses survive, and would have stood at various points within the vallum.

There is a large collection of early Christian grave-slabs and crosses in the Abbey Museum and St Ronan's Church.

The tiny St Columba's Shrine, attached to the cathedral, may be an early medieval oratory, possibly ninth- or tenth-century in date.

Reilig Odhráin is traditionally the burial place of a large number of early Scottish, Irish and Norse kings.

Tòrr an Aba is reputedly the site of Columba's own cell.

Port na Curaich in the south of the island is reputedly the spot where Columba first set foot on Iona.
The Abbey itself as it stands is of thirteenth century and later date.
NM 286245

Kildalton Cross, Islay (P). One of the most complete high crosses in Scotland, similar in date and decoration to the Iona crosses. The cross is in the graveyard of Kildalton Parish Church.
NR 458508

Eileach an Naoimh, Garvellachs. The most complete remains surviving in Scotland of an early Christian monastery. There are stone-built beehive cells, a grave enclosure and a larger enclosure. Access to this isolated

uninhabited island is difficult, requiring boat hire from Tobernochy, Luing and good weather.
NM 640097

Tirefour Broch, Lismore. One of the very few brochs in Argyll. The walls survive to 5m in height, and the Iron Age broch is in an impressive situation.
NM 867429

Clach Ard, Tote, Skye (P). One of the few Pictish symbol stones on the west coast. Probably seventh century.
NG 421491

Kintyre

Kildonan Dun (P). A well-preserved D-shaped dun with staircases within the walls. Excavation provided evidence of occupation in the Iron Age and early medieval periods. Access from a Forest Enterprise car park.
NR 780277

Knapdale

Keills Chapel (P). Many interesting grave-slabs, including early medieval examples, have been collected in the disused chapel.
NR 690805

Kilmory Oib (P). Deserted village with holy well and early stone cross. Signposted from Forest Enterprise car park.
NR 781902

Lorn

Dunollie Castle, Oban. The present ruined castle sits on the site of one of the most important forts of the early medieval period, probably the royal seat of the rulers of the Cenèl Loairne. It was attacked and destroyed several times in the late seventh and eighth centuries. It has a commanding position overlooking Oban Bay and the Sound of Mull. There is little to be seen of the early fort, but excavations revealed similar artefacts to those at Dunadd.
NM 852314

Mid Argyll

Dunadd Fort (HS). The most important fort of Dál Riata, the inauguration place of the Dalriadan kings. There is a series of massive walled enclosures on the upper terraces of the crag, a well and a souterrain. On the summit there are important carvings: a boar, an ogham inscription, a bowl, and a footprint. Excavations revealed large quantities of finds, including metalworking debris from a brooch workshop, and rare imports from Europe. Occupation lasted from the early Iron Age till the tenth century AD.
NR 836935

Kilmartin (P).

Kilmartin Church. There is one early medieval cross in the Church, as well as an important collection of early and later medieval carved grave slabs in a building in the churchyard.
Kilmartin House Museum and Visitor Centre. An innovative and award-winning interpretation centre for the Kilmartin area, with an excellent audio-visual display, a new museum and experimental reconstructions of artefacts.
NR 834988

Perthshire

Scottish Crannog Centre, Kenmore, Loch Tay (P). There is a visitor centre and a reconstructed Iron Age crannog, based on recent underwater excavations in the loch. The reconstruction gives a good idea of what life on a crannog would have been like.
NN 7744

Further Reading

- *Picts, Gaels and Scots,* S. Foster (Batsford/Historic Scotland 1997)
- *Celtic Christianity and Nature:* Early Irish and Hebridean Traditions, M. Low (Edinburgh University Press 1996)
- *The Archaeology of Argyll,* edited by G. Ritchie (Edinburgh University Press 1997)
- *Adomnan of Iona. Life of St Columba,* R. Sharpe (Penguin Classics 1995)

Acknowledgements

I am grateful to the following organisations and individuals for permission to reproduce illustrations, and particularly to Kilmartin House Trust for the use of David Lyons' photographs:

Historic Scotland; Royal Commission of the Ancient and Historical Monuments of Scotland (RCAHMS); National Museums of Scotland; Cardiff University; the Board of Trinity College Dublin; the Bodleian Library, University of Oxford; Royal Irish Academy, Dublin.

I am particularly grateful to those colleagues who discussed in detail a draft of this book, David Broun, Thomas Clancy and Katherine Forsyth, and also to Steve Driscoll, Alex Woolf, Simon Taylor and Alan Lane for discussion and information. Thanks also to Gordon Barclay and Chris Morris for encourgement to write this book, to David Hogg for many interesting discussions on the illustrations, and to Mairi Sutherland for editorial comment. Finally thanks to Rachel, Helen and Chris for providing such a wonderful environment in which to write this book.

Historic Scotland safeguards Scotland's built heritage, including its archaeology, and promotes its understanding and enjoyment on behalf of the Secretary of State for Scotland. It undertakes a programme of 'rescue archaeology', from which many of the results are published in this book series.

Scotland has a wealth of ancient monuments and historic buildings, ranging from prehistoric tombs and settlements to remains from the Second World War, and Historic Scotland gives legal protection to the most important, guarding them against damaging changes or destruction. Historic Scotland gives grants and advice to the owners and occupiers of these sites and buildings.

Historic Scotland has a membership scheme which allows access to properties in its care, as well as other benefits. For information, contact: 0131 668 8999

Dunadd

Dunadd from the air looking towards Crinan and Jura.

KILMARTIN HOUSE TRUST/DAVID LYONS

In memory of my wife
Susan Hakes (1958–1998)